The NLP Master Practitioner Manual

Peter Freeth

CGW
PUBLISHING

2012

The NLP Master Practitioner Manual

First Edition: October 2012

ISBN 978-1-9082932-1-3

CGW Publishing 2012

CGW Publishing

B1502

PO Box 15113

Birmingham

B2 2NJ

www.cgwpublishing.com

mail@cgwpublishing.com

For Stevie, who taught me
everything useful that I
know today

A Model of Excellence

Exercises

In Pursuit of Excellence

A few years ago, I listened to a program on BBC Radio 4 about the time and motion men of the 1950s. Time and motion was a study of efficiency, concluding that much time was lost in movement. By rearranging the stages of a manufacturing process, the process would work more efficiently, productivity would improve, production costs would fall and profits would increase.

The program focused on a British engineering company where craftsmen fabricated turbine blades for jet engines.

This was an incredibly delicate operation, because even the slightest error would cause a vibration which could literally tear the engine apart.

The time and motion men observed the craftsmen carefully, comparing their actions to the company's written procedure. The craftsman took the blade from the foundry, checked it with a micrometer, corrected the blade's width by a fraction of an inch, checked again, corrected again, and so on.

Hundreds of micrometer measurements were required to produce blades that met the strict quality requirements, and the entire process took one whole working day.

The time and motion men went away and reported that the craftsman was working exactly 'by the book', and that the time required to fabricate one blade was, indeed, one day.

Everyone was very happy with this result.

Once the time and motion men had left, the craftsman put away his micrometer and went back to his real method - to check the blade by touch. Running his fingers along the length of the blade, he could detect surface irregularities and other casting defects that were far beyond the capability of a micrometer. The micrometer could only measure the width of the blade at a specific point, and hundreds of measurements were required to 'map' the surface of the blade. The craftsman could essentially feel the entire surface in one movement, and his sense of touch had become very much attuned to the 'right' dimensions, much like a classic car owner knows when something is wrong, simply because the engine's sound changes to such a small degree that no-one else can hear the difference. Even today, craftsmen at Steinway shape the components of a piano by touch rather than by measurement, such is their experience in discriminating the smallest imperfections.

At least in the way that we process sensory signals, our brains are 'difference engines', like the early computers, attuned to changes. The more accustomed we become to something, the more easily we can detect even the slightest variation from the norm.

Using his sense of touch only, the craftsman could produce a finished blade, not in a day, but in half an hour.

Did he use this remarkable talent to increase productivity by 1600%?

No, he spent the rest of the day fishing in the local canal.

As was popular at the time, the company had a well established apprenticeship scheme, where young, inexperienced engineers worked alongside the craftsmen to learn their skills.

Did the apprentice go fishing too?

No, he stayed in the workshop in case the foreman came down to see what was going on.

Did he use that time to reflect on what he had learned from the craftsman?

No, because he didn't know what the craftsman could feel. He knew that the craftsman was feeling something, but it would take him years to learn the skill. That was why apprenticeship schemes were so popular. The philosophy was that you can't teach someone to be a craftsman in five minutes, and there are lots of things that craftsmen do that are very difficult to quantify. Since human beings are outstanding natural learners, the apprenticeship system was an excellent way to train new craftsmen.

The apprenticeship system does have one major flaw.

Have you noticed what happens when a parent says something they shouldn't in front of a young child? The child picks up on it straight away and repeats it, over and over, much to the parent's embarrassment.

Similarly, apprentices didn't only learn the craftsman's technical skills, they learned all of their work avoidance skills too.

I served a three year apprenticeship in the telecoms industry. During that time, I learned how to run cables through a factory or office, I learned to memorise a colour scheme for 200 wires, I learned to solve various technical and mechanical problems and I learned about the theory of communication technologies.

I also learned how to hide private mileage on a company van, what time to expect the area manager, where to get the best bacon sandwiches and how to do 'foreigners', private jobs, using company materials and equipment.

The problem is that you get all or nothing; you can't select only the skills and knowledge that you want to pass on.

Or can you?

Part of the problem is that what we might call 'low value skills' are passed on very easily and can therefore be isolated and taught. The series of steps to connect up a cable, for example.

A public telecoms operator had a written, twelve step procedure for connecting up a cable, however someone noticed that an experienced engineer only performed nine of these steps. Should they therefore rewrite the procedure?

No. The experienced engineer still performed all twelve steps. The difference was that he carried out three of them *inside his head*.

Learning the nine visible steps is easy. What makes the difference between a properly connected cable that will withstand corrosion is contained within those three hidden steps. Those three steps lead to excellence, and you can't see it just by watching. What's more frustrating is that when you ask the person how they are able to excel, they say, "I don't know, I just do it. It's obvious, isn't it?"

The difference between average performance and excellence seems hidden, innate, tacit, impenetrable.

Yet if that were true, this book would not exist.

One of the greatest challenges in businesses today is the protection of tacit knowledge. As competitive pressures increase and a more rapidly changing workforce needs to rely more and more on knowledge that has taken a lifetime to acquire, the ability of HR and L&D professionals to protect an organisation's culture and replicate that unique knowledge has become vital to a business' survival.

Part of a company's market value is defined as its unique knowledge, its "know-how", and as each new generation of graduates spends less and less time in a job, that knowledge must be protected and preserved if its value is to be retained.

For example, one of the UK's oldest and most respected engineering companies had a rapidly ageing workforce in a rapidly changing global market. Their most senior technical staff had designed the first nuclear power stations, military installations and materials handling systems, but within the next five years, 50% of that experience would be lost through retirement.

Attracting new talent was not an issue; the biggest problem was getting the right people into the right places as quickly as possible to 'absorb' that knowledge before it was lost forever.

A British High Street retailer launched a new graduate program, and I used the performance modelling methodology contained within this book to figure out what the highest performers were doing. The results were something of a surprise to the HR team, because the highest performing store managers, buyers and finance managers, in both hard business metrics and staff satisfaction surveys, weren't doing what they were 'supposed' to be doing.

For example, the company had invested considerably in teaching fashionable new 'coaching skills' to the store managers. I discovered that the average store managers relied heavily on their coaching skills, but the high performers used a rather different set of skills.

The HR team adopted my recommendations, with the result that the new graduate program delivered operationally ready staff into the business in just 9 months instead of 12; a 25% saving in time and cost.

The retention of people is a key issue for HR managers and business leaders, but the real, underlying issue isn't the retention of people, it's the retention of tacit knowledge. Abstracting this hard-earned experience from the people who acquired it first hand means that you can develop new talent more quickly and more efficiently, and it means that you can build business processes that automatically favour and align with high performers.

This book explains the methodology behind these outstanding results and shows you how to identify and model your high performers and then use the results in the design and delivery of anything from recruitment and selection processes, interviewing and induction training to performance management, talent management, succession planning and mentoring schemes.

Being a NLP Master Practitioner doesn't mean that you know more techniques than a Practitioner, despite what many of today's NLP trainers would have you believe. A Master Practitioner would ideally use none of the Practitioner techniques – or at least, you'd struggle to see them doing so. A Master Practitioner is most skilled in working conversationally, detecting patterns and making subtle linguistic interventions which simply have the same structure as the Practitioner techniques and are uniquely adapted to each individual client.

Excellence isn't a gift or an accident, it's something that people work hard to achieve. They may not set out to achieve it, they may not even realise that they have achieved it, yet by stopping, watching and listening, you'll discover the secrets to all kinds of talents, and they'll rarely be what you thought they would be.

The NLP Master Practitioner Manual will help you to discover those secrets, work more elegantly and discreetly with your clients and go far beyond anything that you thought you knew about NLP.

2

We Are Simulators

You have probably been on a motion simulator at a funfair. It might have featured a roller-coaster ride, or a runaway train, or a jet fighter performing aerobatics. The machine itself is just a combination of two things; a video, taking from the participant's eye view, and a 'motion platform' that shakes you about in time with the movie.

However enjoyable these rides may be, you're very unlikely to believe that you actually were on a real roller-coaster. However, what is most fascinating about these machines is that they can simulate so many different activities. The operator just puts in a different DVD and a spaceship is transformed into an airboat, skimming over Florida's Everglades. The simulation is good enough for most people to suspend reality just long enough to enjoy the ride.

Professional flight simulators are something quite different. They take an actual cockpit from the aircraft in question and place it within the motion platform. Incredibly complex and detailed graphics simulate any airport, complete with the right aircraft and vehicles on the ground, weather, terrain and feedback through the aircraft's cockpit displays. These simulators are so accurate that when a pilot crashes one, the stress is as severe as if the aircraft were real, and time in a simulator is equivalent to time in the air, as far as licensing is concerned.

After half an hour in a flight simulator, you would definitely be forgiven for forgetting that you were never more than thirty feet from the ground.

Meteorologists spend much of their time gathering data from weather stations. On top of buildings, at airports and out on remote hillsides, monitoring stations collect data on wind speed and direction, rainfall, temperature and humidity. Why are they so interested in collecting such useless data? Is it just so that they can tell us that it's been the wettest July since 1903?

No. The reason that they collect this data is so that they can constantly refine and update their weather models. By comparing their simulations to actual conditions, they can increase their confidence in their predictions. The scientist Nikola Tesla was said to construct mental models that he ran alongside his physical experiments. He would lock his experiments in a room and after many days or even months, discover that the physical experiment matched his mental simulation perfectly.

This shouldn't be surprising, though, because you can do exactly the same thing. You can put some bread under the grill and go into another room. The phone rings, you end up chatting, you forget about the toast and when you start to smell smoke, you instantly know what you're going to find under the grill. How surprised would you be if you *didn't* find two smouldering squares of charcoal?

And when you return to a favourite restaurant or holiday destination, how do you feel when it's not how you remembered it?

Sometimes, you criticise yourself. It might be when you feel you have made an obvious mistake, or it might be when you knew you should have listened to your intuition but didn't.

One of the first things that most people learn in NLP training is how to listen to and modify their internal dialogue. You learn to hear the sound of your father or mother chastising you and modify it to be a carton character or newsreader, with the effect that you don't feel so bad about the mistake you made.

This doesn't work in the real world. If you are cornered in a dark alley by a knife wielding thug, imagining him with a clown's nose might alleviate the tension but it doesn't change the fact that he's after your money.

We build simulations that mirror reality so that we can predict what will happen in reality and take action to achieve our goals and avoid danger.

Imagine that someone throws a snowball at you. Given enough time, you can intuitively compute the snowball's flight path and move your head out of the way, just in time. This is an incredibly complex thing to be able to do, and it cannot be achieved by reacting, because by the time you react, the snowball is no longer where it was when you saw it.

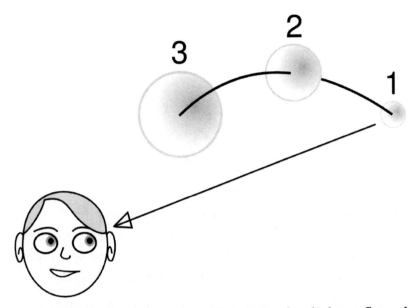

When the snowball is in position 1, the light reflected from it arrives at your eyes almost instantly, but the signal from your retinas takes a much longer period of time to reach your brain, by which time the snowball, which is moving at a fairly constant speed, is in position 2. Your brain takes time to process the visual information, compute the snowball's path, determine in which direction to move to avoid the snowball and begin signalling to your muscles through your motor cortex, by which time the snowball is in position 3.

By the time your muscles begin to respond, the snowball is now in this position:

After you have recovered, you will probably feel a little silly that you saw the snowball but couldn't get out of the way fast enough to avoid it. No matter how good your reactions are, you can never overcome this signal delay.

When you think about the computation required to recognise a fast moving object as an incoming icy missile, determine its path, calculate avoiding action and then translate that action into specific muscle movements, it's a wonder that you get to see the snowball at all.

Having a good reaction time simply means that you don't have to think about what to do for as long, but there is nothing that you can do about that signal delay. By the time you are processing the image of the snowball, it has already moved further along its flight path, and by the time your muscles begin contracting, it has moved further still.

At a very early age, you learned to simulate the laws of motion. Newton wrote them out in plain English for other people to understand, and from those laws we can now throw snowballs with some degree of accuracy, and we can also launch a spaceship with three men on board, land it on the moon and return it to Earth with only a few minutes of fuel to spare.

If you have read The NLP Practitioner Manual, you may recall that in 2005, NASA launched a probe called Deep Impact that, seven months later, crashed into the "Tempel 1" comet. The comet is essentially a lump of ice, 4 miles across and travelling at about 23,000 mph. The probe was about the size of a washing machine.

NASA's analogy is that the probe hitting the comet is like a pebble hitting a truck. A pebble that you threw seven months ago.

Just imagine that for a moment. You look through a telescope and see a comet, millions of miles away. You observe it every day and, accounting for the time it takes the light reflected from the comet to reach your telescope, you calculate the comet's path, using equations that were developed over 300 years ago in 1687. The Wright brothers didn't achieve sustained, heavier than air flight until more than 200 years later in 1903. Yet you can calculate the path of the comet with such confidence that you can take something the size of a washing machine, place it on top of a very large firework, light the blue touch paper and launch it out beyond Earth's atmosphere where it just floats along at its own pace, obeying Newton's first law of motion until, seven months later, the paths of the comet and the probe intersect.

A certain genre of film associated with martial arts often shows the hero shooting an arrow and knocking an enemy's arrow out of the air. It's utterly implausible, but no less impossible, technically, than a military anti-missile system that can hit something the size of a baguette travelling at 2,600 mph.

The only difference between the film and reality is that computers are much better at computing flight paths, quickly, than most humans are.

Remember, the purpose of a simulation is to be able to predict the future.

When people act inappropriately, or they act in a certain way because of the reaction that they hope to get, they are trying to control future events. If I want to open a door, I can predict the amount of force with which to push or pull it. I try to control the future behaviour of the door in order to achieve an outcome.

A child learns to control future events by asking for more pocket money when Daddy's watching the football, or Mummy's on the phone. But parents can "wise up" to these early attempts at manipulation, and the child has to revise its simulations.

We cannot ever get away from simulations because they literally make us who we are. However, what we can seek to do is narrow the gap between our simulations and reality, just like the meteorologists do, and this is the goal of NLP.

Creating a simulation of an inanimate object, moving within the consistent and predictable 'laws' of physics isn't that difficult. We know this because we can program computers to make predictions based on the constants that govern the motion of objects, gravity, the behaviour of gases as their temperature changes and so on. But humans are quite different; their behaviour based on a far more complex set of rules and constants. Humans seem to change over time, they seem to make different choices in the same situation from one day to the next and they adapt to changes in the external environment.

Philosophers have, over many thousands of years, attempted to understand human behaviour, coming up with various theories to define this experience that we call "reality". Yet, intuitively, we have each mastered the ability to predict the complexities of "human nature". You walk into a bar to meet a friend and correctly order a drink for them, even when it's not what they normally have. A parent preempts their child's behaviour and prevents an embarrassing situation at a restaurant. You weigh up a dilemma and the mentor on your shoulder gives you exactly the advice that they would offer if they were sitting in front of you.

I'm sure you've had this latter experience. Your hand reaches for the chocolate and a voice in the back of your head reminds you of the promise you made to yourself. Whose voice is it? We build simulations of people close to us that are so lifelike that they often seem to take on a life of their own, giving direction, advice and criticism as if the person was there in the room with you.

Children need to acquire their parents' experiences in order to stay safe. They need to learn boundaries and in order to operate independently as responsible adults, they need to live by those rules without they parent watching over their every move. But we often inherit more rules from our parents than we would like, and it can be difficult for some people to separate the useful rules from those which have become outdated.

One of the aspects of mental simulation that is most often cited in the self-help world is mental rehearsal. The idea is that by running through a scenario in your mind, you can develop the same level of skill as if you were really practising it. Taken to extremes, some celebrity self-help gurus talk about the "law" of attraction, which means that by harbouring positive thoughts, you can 'manifest' wealth and happiness into your life. Sadly, such claims discredit the underlying science which is regularly used by athletes when they rehearse for races. They can't control what their opponents will do on the day, but they can rehearse the track in their minds until every twist and turn is 'second nature' to them.

What is the reality of mental rehearsal? Does it simply build a memory of a task, or does it affect the body too? When people are asked to imagine a task while in a MRI scanner, the results show that many brain areas are engaged just as they would be in the physical performance of that task. But surely, this doesn't affect someone's muscles. How could it? Yet research conducted by Alvaro Pascual-Leone indicates that practice not only reinforces a person's memory of a task, it also enlarges the brain's motor area for the muscles that control that task. More output neurons means stronger muscles and better muscle control. Pascual-Leone used a technology called TMS (Transcranial Magentic Stimulation) to map brain activity in great detail. In a study of people learning to play the piano, he compared people practising at a real keyboard with people who were simply *imagining* playing. After five days, the 'mental' players required only a two hour live practice session to acquire the same level of skill as the people who had practised on a real keyboard.

In another study, Drs Yue and Cole compared a group of people undertaking physical exercise with a group who just imagined exercising. At the end of the four week study, the people who had physically exercised had increased their muscle strength by 30%. Surprisingly, the people who had only *imagined* the same exercise increased their muscle strength by 22%.

We mustn't get carried away with such news; while mental rehearsal can strengthen the brain's connections to muscles, the muscles themselves don't change, and you certainly won't 'think yourself thin'. However, when learning fine motor tasks such as are involved in sports or music, mental rehearsal clearly benefits the learning process.

In 2000, I worked as a teacher for a 'gifted and talented' project, running weekend and holiday courses for young children. On one course, a number of the children said that they wanted to be able to use a computer keyboard more quickly, so I tried an experiment. Their starting level of ability was to type with the index finger of their dominant hand, with a few seconds delay between key presses while they searched around the keyboard for the key they wanted. I theorised that, once they had found a letter, they didn't forget where it was. The reason that they searched for each letter was that they only *thought* they didn't know which letters were in which location, when at some unconscious level, they intuitively knew. In fact, young children can easily acquire 'procedural knowledge', enabling them to learn a task, but only when their brains have further developed can they articulate that knowledge. So intuitively knowing the location of a letter on a keyboard but not being able to translate that into the sound or word would probably make sense.

I gave the children a series of very simple, repetitive tasks to perform. First, I had them typing rows and rows of letters in the order that they appear on the keyboard; QWERTY... After a few minutes, the children's' typing got faster and settled into a comfortable rhythm, so I changed the task to typing the letters in alphabetical order; ABCDE... Again, their typing was slow at first but soon accelerated and settled into a rhythm. I then changed the task to 'the quick brown fox...' and this time, as they practised typing, I distracted them by saying the alphabet backwards, counting and so on. What happened was quite remarkable; the more I distracted them, the faster they could type.

I then let them rest, and then had them imagine typing, and asked them to imagine themselves in different scenarios; at school, at home, with friends, typing letters, emails, and perhaps most importantly, receiving positive comments, praise and supportive feedback. Finally, I had them physically practice again. All of the children, a group of about 15, showed a marked increase in the speed and accuracy of their typing and, perhaps most importantly, their confidence that they *could* type.

Clearly, the more accurate and challenging the mental simulations we can build, the more we can achieve the ultimate goal of all self-help gurus; *to fulfil our potential.*

Brainy People

You are a very brainy person. In fact, we could even go so far as to say that you are one big brain. Every part of your body has evolved to serve the needs of your brain. Your senses gather external information and your muscles enable your brain to modify external events so that your sensory experience aligns with your desires.

Imagine, for a moment, a drink. Something that you want, perhaps a cup of tea or coffee. As you imagine it, you know exactly what to do in order to get it. By conjuring up that mental simulation, your entire neurology and physiology can spring into action to close the gap between desire and reality.

Most NLP books and training programs contain some descriptions of neurology and brain organisation. Personally, I believe that when Bandler and Grinder first created NLP, Bandler wanted to hijack some real science in order to lend NLP some credibility, just like some alternative therapists maintain that the law of attraction is based on the real science of quantum mechanics.

Seriously, it's utter nonsense. And you know it, don't you?

The problem with NLP trainers who talk about neurology is that they are regurgitating knowledge that is at least forty years old, and of course they are largely regurgitating a rather one sided account of that knowledge which has more to do with NLP's early brand image than any real science.

I don't want you thinking that you only get upset because your amygdala takes over, or that your ancient reptilian brain is where all of your base desires live. This model of brain function is closer to the Victorian art of phrenology than to any modern understanding of brain science, even though it is still being taught on self-styled accelerated learning courses. By the way, why does it take three days to learn about accelerated learning?And why is there a book entitled, "Speed reading in a week". Shouldn't that be "Speed reading in five minutes"?

Even twenty years ago, a theory of 'holographic' brain function was emerging, where functions are spread across the brain rather than localised in particular areas. Even those localised areas are named, not after any understanding of their function, but after the person who first dissected them or the animal that they remind someone of. Your hippocampus is so named because it looks a bit like a seahorse. I suppose we should think our selves lucky that our neural structures are not shaped like anything more embarrassing.

We cannot figure out how the mind works by dissecting it, however there is another approach that we can learn from, and that is the approach taken by the people who are trying not to figure out how the brain *works* but to reproduce what it *does*.

Artificial Intelligence is one goal of computer research, however there seems to be some disagreement over what intelligence is, even though we can be fairly certain what the 'artificial' part refers to. Or can we? Robots have been built that use cells from rat brains to make navigational decisions, and electronic components have been inserted into peoples' bodies, and I'm not just talking about the assistant at the local electrical retailer who told me that they couldn't replace the mobile phone that I bought last week because it's already obsolete. No, I'm talking about people who have had artificial retinas and ear drums wired into their brains.

One of the most interesting people in this field of research is Steve Grand, who set out to build an artificial orang-utan called Lucy. His goal was to have Lucy point at a banana.

Now, this in itself is a very simple task. We can easily program a computer to recognise the characteristic shape and colour of a banana, under controlled conditions, and we can easily have that computer control a robotic arm to 'point' at that banana. You might have a digital camera that has 'face recognition' so that the camera can focus on the nearest face, even if it isn't centred in the frame. But that does not make your camera intelligent, it merely emulates one tiny aspect of your abilities, and that idea is central to the way that Steve Grand is approaching the problem. He built Lucy 'from the ground up', from first principles. Rather than building a robot to *do* something, such as paint a car or mow your lawn, he built Lucy to emulate the way that our brains are wired up, and in doing so, he figured out some very interesting functions that relate to our simulation theory of mind.

Since Steve Grand probably isn't interested in NLP, and since most neuroscience authors probably aren't interested in Steve's attempts to build a mechanical monkey in his garage, it falls to us to bridge the gap between these two fascinating and complementary areas of research.

For a long time, there has been a theory of brain function that represents the brain as a number of discrete functional areas. Visual processing here, right index finger there, sense of self awareness down in that corner. This model essentially developed from the study of one man, Phineas Gage, who we'll discuss later on. In short, he suffered a serious brain injury but survived, minus some aspects of his personality. This demonstrated that the bits of mental facility that he lost were resident in the bits of brain that were blown out of the top of his head by a large metal rod, and fitted very nicely with the observation that the rest of the human body is also made up of clearly delineated functional areas called organs.

However, as medical science has progressed, we no longer need to remove parts of the brain in order to deduce function, we can watch the brain in action in real time by giving people tasks and observing which parts of their brain draw more oxygen from blood flow, indicating increased activity and therefore functional significance.

I should point out that the latest neurological old wives' tale that is doing the rounds is that when you connect an EEG machine to a strawberry jelly, it shows the same signs of consciousness as are observed in the human brain. Therefore, to deduce brain function by observing brain operation is misleading at best. By the way, I cannot find any evidence of this supposed research, and it seems likely that it's an urban myth, like the early experiments into subliminal messaging which are often the subject of discussion on NLP training courses. By the time you read this, it will probably be 'common knowledge' that strawberry jelly is sentient, according to the neurologists whose statistical analysis of random electrical activity leaves them clutching at straws in an effort to prove that they can determine a person's thoughts from the electrical activity in their brains. You can mock them now, but when the fruit trifles move in and take all our women and jobs, you'll be laughing on the other side of your face.

We now know that the brain is made up, not of functional organs, but of layers. Every sensory nerve ending in your body arrives, through your brain stem, into a primary input area, and every motor nerve leaves your brain through a primary output area.

In that regard, we humans are no different, neurologically, from any other animal; from earthworms to orang-utans. The key difference between ourselves and other animals is not the number of brain cells that we have, nor the number of chromosomes in our DNA; it is the number of processing steps that a signal goes through in between reception and action. Each of these processing steps could introduce an extra layer of finesse or detail into the overall decision process.

When a shadow passes over a frog, it dives for cover. It doesn't differentiate between a kestrel and a pigeon, as it simply reacts to a pattern of changing light levels. This means that a frog can react much faster than a human because there are fewer layers of processing in between 'shadow' and 'jump'. Similarly, if you have ever tried to swat a fly, you'll know that they excel at moving out of the way, just when you think you have them cornered. This isn't because the fly 'thinks' any faster than you do, it's simply to do with those previously mentioned signal delays. An external observer will see that the fly has already moved out of the way before your hand is anywhere near it, thanks to its short reception to action delay, and you're unable to adjust your action because you don't even know that the fly has moved. When you swat a fly with a rolled up newspaper, it's smaller than your hand but it's also moving a lot faster, and as long as you attack the fly from the same direction as it is flying towards, the result will be bad news for the fly.

Whilst frogs and flies can react faster than humans, they lack our versatility, and most importantly they lack our ability to understand and predict possible future events. If a predator approached you, you would have a number of choices available; freeze, run, grab a stick, try to distract it or even negotiate with it if the predator in question is a sales assistant in a furniture store. This versatility requires complex computational power, and that comes at the expense of raw speed.

Probably the most recognisable part of the human brain is the cortex, which is essentially a folded sheet of nerve tissue wrapped around the central parts of the brain. It's as if those original parts grew more and more layers, so those layers became folded in order to pack them inside your skull, much like a folded umbrella manages to pack a large surface area into an apparently small volume.

At the centre of all of this is a structure called the Superior Colliculus, through which all incoming and outgoing nerve connections are routed. One important observation which reinforces the theories that I'm covering here is that the more complex the behavioural response, the further into the cortex are the connections that drive that behaviour.

For example, fundamental behaviours such as breathing and regulating a heart beat are driven from within the brain stem itself. Our version of the frog's "Leg it!" response is called our 'orienting response', and it automatically points your eyes in the direction of movement. Crucially, the computational work required to achieve this feat never gets any further than the Superior Colliculus, so by the time you are consciously aware of what you are looking at, your eyes have already been pointing at it for some time. A similar response orients your eyes in the direction of new sounds. Just imagine for a moment the calculations required to achieve that, and remember that all of that takes place in the most basic area of your brain. Your brain takes two images or sounds which arrive at different angles, tracks changing signal levels across a two dimensional surface (your retina), computes a three dimensional location, translates that into a two dimensional muscle movement and then continues to track that changing signal over time as the object in question moves across your visual field.

Cortex

Superior Colliculus

Brainstem

In the image above, you can see the folded or 'convoluted' cortex, wrapped around the central areas of the brain. Those layers are pretty much the same, regardless of which part of the cortex we look at, which is very interesting indeed, and certainly fits with what we know of the brain's 'plasticity'; its ability to reorganise itself in case of damage. Nerve tissue apparently never regrows, but the brain can move functions around in order to bypass areas that have been damaged by injury or perhaps a stroke.

A typically simplified model of perception that you might learn about on a NLP course looks like this:

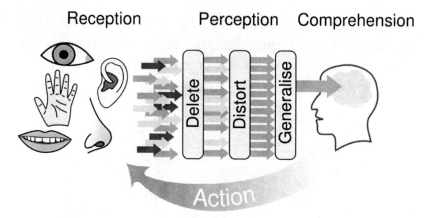

This model implies that perception happens in only one direction, and action also happens only in one direction. If we mapped this simplified model onto the structure of the brain, we might represent the chain of connections as follows:

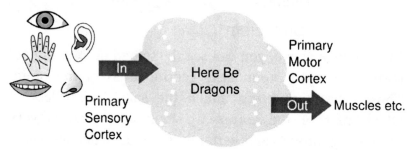

However, our brains are not wired up that way; there are connections running back in the opposite direction too.

The cortex is made up of a number of distinct layers, distinct in that they look different when studied under a microscope. Traditionally, there are six layers, and in some regions of the brain, those six layers are further divided into sub-layers.

The NLP Master Practitioner Manual

Connections can be traced between the layers, and if we take a functional view of the brain rather than a structural one, it would appear that there are in fact four functional layers. A structural view would be to say that because something is built differently, it must be different. A functional view says that because something functions differently, it must be different.

A horse and a car are structurally different but functionally similar. A telephone directory and a romantic novel are structurally similar but functionally different.

A cross section, grouping the six traditional layers into four functional layers, looks like the diagram on the right.

Each layer of the brain looks like some kind of transport interchange, not with a simple 'in' and 'out' but with connections both in and out at both the 'top' and the 'bottom'. But what purpose could these extra connections possibly serve?

The answer might be found within the mysterious region of the model where 'thinking' happens, whatever that means. Unlike frogs and earthworms,

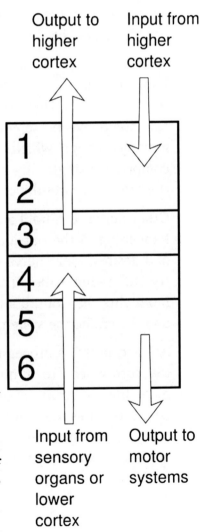

Output to higher cortex

Input from higher cortex

1
2
3
4
5
6

Input from sensory organs or lower cortex

Output to motor systems

we do not react to the outside world directly, we react to a simulation of it, and that simulation contains what we could call our 'desired state'. Whilst our eyes may orient themselves automatically towards movement, our 'higher functions' such as being able to identify a moving object, determine if it poses a threat and decide what to do about it are most definitely influenced by factors such as past experiences and current emotional state. A very simplified description of the theory is as follows.

Within our brains, nerve cells hold a copy of what is happening in the outside world, as sampled through our sensory organs. They work like an old fashioned cathode ray tube television screen, holding a complete, apparently moving image which at any given instant really only comprises a single tiny dot of light, moving quickly across the screen in carefully organised and synchronised rows.

Other nerve cells hold a copy of what we would like to be happening in the outside world, as defined by our needs and desires. More nerve cells compare the two 'maps' and try to reduce the differences between the two by modifying their outputs to motor systems such as muscles and the endocrine system.

At each layer of processing, the cells and connections in the cortex seek to minimise the difference between the incoming 'present state' signals and the internally connected 'desired state' signals. Just like the thermostat on your central heating, the system takes action to achieve a specific goal, and when that goal has been achieved, the output of the system reduces.

"Reality Map"   Negotiation   "Desire Map"

Motor Output

It's hard to imagine such complexities and subtleties of human behaviour working in such a simple way, until you take into account the fact that, in your brain, there is a nerve 'map' for every nerve ending, every cell on your retina, every taste bud, every muscle and every hair follicle, to name but a few. Those external connections are combined and integrated through these successive layers of processing, until a complex behaviour such as 'drive to the shops' can be de-constructed into a script of muscle movements, sensory inputs and rational decisions that begins with hearing an advert on the radio for a delicious new chocolate bar.

I believe that not only is this the most realistic, practical and accurate model of brain function, it also happens to fit very neatly with other models and theories which are equally practical, such as Gallese and Goldman's Simulation Theory and even Eric Berne's Transactional Analysis.

Steve Grand's work is fascinating because he is not a neurologist and he has not arrived at his design for Lucy by trying to understand the brain but instead by trying to replicate it. Coincidentally, the test of a NLP model is similar; can you reproduce the results of the person whose talent you have modelled?

Another important aspect of these 'backwards' connections is their ability to modify input. As babies develop their neural wiring, they become accustomed to certain inputs, learning to prioritise the importance of different stimuli. We are extremely economical and efficient machines, so neural connections which are not used are erased. A chemical called Oxytocin allows synpatic connections to 'dissolve' and be replaced with new ones, and it is the chemical of both learning and love. Neuroscientists have even theorised that the production of Oxytocin, which increases when we fall in love, allows us to forgive and forget, or at least to forget, by literally dissolving old memories and patterns of behaviour. If you want to change the habit of a lifetime, fall head over heels in love with someone who discourages it.

Our eyes and ears are receptive to a certain range of stimuli. For example, we can see light in a frequency range which we perceive as running from red through to violet. We see the colours of a rainbow, not because they are 'there' but because our eyes detect frequencies of light in a certain way. We know that some insects can see in what we would call the 'ultraviolet' range, and we know that dogs can hear in what we would call the 'ultrasound' range. Our sensory organs have evolved specifically for the purpose of living on Earth, so it's no surprise that both the retinal cells of our eyes and the chlorophyll in plants are optimised for working in sunlight.

When we start to build more complex structures on top of these basic sensory systems, something interesting happens. Language is a good example, because it is so incredibly complex. Our ability to convert an experience into an abstract set of symbols and then convey those symbols to another person – or even a dog – in such a way that the original experience, or something like it, is recreated in the mind of the received is nothing short of miraculous. Our ability to hear language is learned, and our ability to learn is influenced by the production of Oxytocin. If you want to learn a new language, go to classes with someone you love.

While our natural production of Oxytocin declines past childhood, we can restart it by choosing to try out new experiences, keeping our brains active, fit and healthy.

One of the hardest things about learning a new language is hearing the different sounds or phonemes that make up that language. Whilst English and French, for example, have many different words for the same things, the basic sounds of the vowels and consonants are quite similar, and certainly similar enough that you could get through a holiday with a phrase book. But what about English compared to Finnish or Japanese? Some of the phonemes are very different, a stereotypical example being that native Japanese speakers struggle with the sound of the letter 'R', pronouncing it as a 'L'. As a Japanese baby grows, it hears only Japanese language and so its remarkably economical brain develops only the necessary connections. A native Japanese speaker doesn't only struggle with 'R' because they're not used to saying it, they struggle because their brains are unable to process the sound of 'R', so they never develop the connections required to say it. As a baby, they never hear it, so they never develop the connections to make sense of and replicate it. Even within the UK, we struggle to pronounce place names in Scotland and Wales, simply because we're not used to the way that 'LL', 'DD' and 'GH' are used, and many of us struggle to understand the 'broadest' regional accents, simply because we're not used to hearing them. When I lived in the North East of England for a while, I found it very difficult to make myself understood when giving out my telephone number, because the number zero, 'oh', rhymes with 'four'. When I said "four", it would be heard as "oor", meaning zero.

The point here is that these reverse connections modify sensory input in order to simplify processing and cognition. If you were building a computer system to analyse images, such as a car number plate recognition system, you would want to reduce the amount of computational power required as much as possible, because that will optimise the system's response time and accuracy. If you could use a camera which only received light around the yellow range of the visible spectrum, it would emphasise the number plates on the back of British cars and reduce the amount of information for the computer to process.

The sensory capability of our eyes and ears is modified by our experiences so that we become more attuned to seeing and hearing what we expect.

Michael Merzenich is another name worth looking up; he has been working in the field of 'neuroplasticity' for many years and has pioneered a revolution in neurology; a revolution which has shaken the previously accepted model that brain functions are localised into functional areas that cannot be changed once a person leaves their childhood. Merzenich's work shows that the brain reorganises itself surprisingly quickly when recovering from damage or adapting to new experiences. Some of his experiments, and those of others in the field, have involved mapping the individual connections between sensory receptors and the cortex, showing that there is a one to one mapping between the various senses and the processing centres of the brain. For example, there is a topographical map of the skin within the brain, meaning that the map is the same overall shape as the real thing. The area of your brain where your right index finger tip connects to is next to the area where your right thumb tip connects to, however that won't be in precisely the same place as it is in my brain.

You can read more about Merzenich's research in any of his publications or papers, or in 'The Brain that Changes Itself' by Normal Doidge, a popular science book which collects a number of different fields of research to add weight to the argument that the brain never stops growing, changing and learning.

Personally, I find it more surprising that scientists ever believed the brain to be immutable. After all, you are learning from these words as you read them now. Could it really be possible that your brain is acquiring new knowledge *without* changing in some way? Why should learning from a new experience be significantly different to learning a new language or recovering the use of a limb after nerve damage?

Where, you may ask, does this research fit with NLP? The 'desire map' is an obvious analogy for a goal, belief, value, outcome or need. It doesn't really matter which of those words we use, because the end result is the same - an intention to modify the world to meet our expectations. What NLP gives us is two important things:

1. A way to reveal and perhaps modify those hidden behavioural drivers

2. A way to modify the 'desire map' that directs our behaviour and the results that we achieve

We could say that the brain's purpose is to direct external behaviour so that the difference between present and desired state is minimised, but that then raises the question of where the desired state comes from. Sometimes, regardless of what long term plans we make, our short term actions seem to lead us round in circles.

Clearly, certain essential biological processes can drive the desire map; thirst or hunger, for example. But where does a desire map for a promotion or for recognition from one's peers come from?

Steve Grand proposed that our brains comprise layers upon layers of such maps which each have their own short term goals and form part of a larger, far more complex pattern of behaviour. Certainly, we could relate a need for food or security to a job promotion through a chain of connected beliefs. One role of NLP is to challenge those beliefs so that a person may meet their needs more effectively.

The goal of any living organism is homeostasis; an equilibrium that keeps the organism healthy and alive.

Life is a delicate balance, for example between staying in the safety of the cave, risking starvation and heading out to forage, risking being eaten by a predator. Your body temperature, blood oxygenation and stomach acid level must all be maintained within carefully controlled ranges, and either too much or too little can be fatal.

While homeostasis is a good thing at a level of basic bodily functions, it's not so useful for humans with career aspirations and other long term goals, because it tends to keep you exactly where you are. Many psychotherapeutic approaches work with 'life scripts'; behaviours learned during our childhood that are no longer appropriate for us yet which repeat as if on autopilot. We know this when we act like our parents and promise to stop, yet we hear the same words coming out of our mouths as if someone else is in the driving seat.

We need to be able to break the connection between past experiences and future expectations, and having done that, we need to create a new direction and outcome.

NLP isn't the only tool kit that can achieve that end, but it is the only one that is the subject of this book, so for now, we're both stuck with it.

To summarise, the purpose and function of a brain is to minimise the difference between an organism's present and desired states. NLP gives us a set of tools for minimising the differences between that perceived present state and 'objective reality', and also for modifying the desired state so that it reflects our conscious, long term plans rather than our unconscious, learned, repetitive behaviours.

⁴A Word on NLP

This book has evolved out of the workbook for my NLP Master Practitioner training program, and in doing so has become the workbook itself. However, the book also stands by itself as a performance modelling toolkit. You can use it to model high performers, whether or not you have any prior knowledge or opinion of NLP.

Therefore, I should explain something about NLP that will be relevant for anyone who is studying or has studied at Master Practitioner level.

I have seen many Master Practitioner training courses that were packed full of ever more complicated techniques; techniques for this or that kind of phobia, allergy cures, confidence boosters, techniques for getting rid of compulsions, or undesirable memories.

Well, we could say that undesirable memories are what make you who you are. They remind you of things that you regret, mistakes that you know not to repeat. As Virginia Satir said, and I paraphrase, we can't change those things, it's how we respond to them and deal with them that makes the difference.

Probably the biggest concern I have with much of today's NLP Master Practitioner training is that it focuses on more techniques, when techniques are not part of any Master Practitioner certification syllabus that I've ever seen. And if your syllabus is different, then I submit to you that you are missing out on the most important, the most central and the most valuable part of NLP; modelling.

In fact, NLP *is* modelling. Techniques are *not* NLP. They are the *results* of NLP. Therefore, to pay good money for a Master Practitioner training course and not learn modelling means that you have definitely been short-changed. And by modelling, I don't mean strategy elicitation. That's just the first step.

But how can all those NLP trainers be wrong? Well, they're not wrong, just misinformed. They were trained by trainers who didn't know how to model, so they just extended what they did at Practitioner level, which is to throw techniques at the client until either they find one that sticks or the client lose the will to live and says that they're all better now, thank you for your help. Modelling can be laborious; it took Bandler and Grinder many months to analyse and code what they had learned from Erickson. Meanwhile, techniques are sexy and fulfil the 'quick fix' need that brings many students to NLP. For coaches who want to be able to wave a magic wand, spending hours breaking down and analysing a talent, even a self defeating one, doesn't seem worth the effort.

This chain of events goes back many generations, in terms of NLP training, and I think that we can say that there are a number of causes for the resulting shortfall in Master Practitioner standards:

- Most NLP trainers don't understand how to model

- Many NLP trainers want to show off by doing lots of cool techniques

- Some NLP trainers aren't very good at NLP, so complicated techniques are a neat smokescreen

The NLP Master Practitioner certification syllabus is all about modelling, because modelling is the process by which we create techniques. We model someone who used to be scared of public speaking and now isn't and we create an anti-stage fright technique. If we generalise the model enough, it will work for most people. But it will never work for everyone. No NLP technique will work for everyone, because not everyone fits the generalised model. If we generalise a model to the degree that it fits everyone, it's now too vague to be useful to anyone.

I've mentioned the certification criteria at Master Practitioner level, so you're probably wondering what those criteria are, in full.

NLP Master Practitioner

- Multi-level tasking and purposeful multi-level communication, including:

- Detect conscious and unconscious communication.

- Distinguish between content and structure.

- Understand and integrate the presuppositions of NLP.

- Understand remedial and generative change.

- Customising NLP Practitioner techniques to meet the needs of a client.

- Creating states of consciousness and physiology that lead to flexibility and creativity in thinking and action.

- Making conscious shifts in perspective, state and behaviour to maintain overall control of the coaching process.

Meta Programs

- Elicit Meta Programs and build them into your coaching approach.

Framing outcomes

[handwritten: "mastery" (well formed) ↓]

✓ Understand the difference between an <u>outcome</u> and a direction. *(generative)*

[handwritten: (structured) + (sustainable)]

Have a systemic approach to predicting the implications of change over time. *[handwritten: ie, pre-empting barriers, challenges resistance, and opportunities]*

[handwritten left margin: the process of mastery]

✓ Generalise change through time. *[handwritten: convincers / unfolding, prepare for unexpected scenario / future pace to plan for future events, circumstance / extrapolating]*

Advanced Language Skills

✗ Detect Sleight of Mouth Patterns. *[handwritten: decoding language / deconstructing language]*

✗ Reframing at different logical levels using the various Sleight of Mouth Patterns. *[handwritten: using meta model]*

✓ Sort incongruities and integrate them conversationally. *[handwritten: (sleuthing)]*

[handwritten: notice]

✓ Implement the patterns of NLP techniques conversationally, e.g. through presuppositions in questions. *[handwritten: ex: Peter + Steve H]*

[handwritten: • Imagine you're a fly on the wall ; that dissociates / • what do you think about / • think about it → Think al running / Think about running / Imagine running]

Values and Criteria

✓ Elicit values for the purpose of motivation, setting outcomes, negotiation procedures, conflict resolution, etc. *[handwritten: whats important, what their drivers are]*

Advanced Strategies Skills

✓ Elicit, design, modify and install strategies.

[handwritten: your desire the reason Your rationale]

✓ Use motivation, convincer, decision, and follow through strategies inside other techniques. *[handwritten: what happened   whats next?]*

[handwritten: how they are different]

Trance

Recognise, induce, and utilise naturally occurring trance phenomena, also known as conversational hypnosis.

Developing a greater awareness and utilisation of a systemic approach.

As you can see, no techniques. "Ah!", you say, "But reframing is a technique!" No. Reframing is a class of technique and also an aspect of every technique. Every NLP technique reframes. Every NLP technique changes a pattern. Every NLP technique changes the submodalities of the client's experience with regard to the 'problem'. These are broad definitions of how NLP works, not narrow techniques that you 'do' to someone.

NLP is not about the techniques at all. You could regard the techniques as being a useful prop for beginners, a collection of mystical incantations for intermediate Practitioners or a set of scripts for people who are afraid to improvise.

For the most talented Practitioners, you could regard the techniques as something that they do to show the client that they're doing something, while in reality all of the change work has already been done, conversationally. After all, who in their right minds would pay good money for a peculiar handshake and a five minute chat that leaves you feeling oddly positive about something that you're certain had been troubling you, if only you could remember what it had been, isn't it?

If you enjoy quoting Bandler, then remember that he says, "NLP is an attitude and a methodology that leaves behind a trail of techniques."

Note that he has not been recorded as saying, "NLP is a set of cool techniques."

This book is about the methodology, with a bit of attitude thrown in for good measure. The techniques are up to you.

⁵Development

Another valuable way of understanding how people learn is by understanding how our brains and mental abilities developed. Through experiment, we are able to deduce how children see the world differently to most adults, and we can therefore see the stages of learning from a different angle.

How do we know what children think?

Children take a relatively long time to develop to full mental maturity. Humans, as a species, are unusual in that our babies are unable to fend for themselves when born. Many other mammals can stand and walk within minutes of birth, but because humans have a relatively large head, a human baby is born with a brain that is not yet fully developed.

Our mental capacity comes at the cost of an extended development phase after we are born, when we are extremely vulnerable and need the protection of our parents and other adults. Many months of learning must pass before a human baby can do the things that a lamb or calf can do almost immediately after birth.

This extended developmental period gives psychologists an opportunity to study how children learn, how they perceive the world, how they think and how they develop.

The Swiss scientist Jean Piaget conducted extensive research and described a number of development stages that a child will normally progress through, and these form the basis for much of child psychology and developmental testing today.

Learning by doing

Children live in a concrete, sensory world. If you have ever played a game of 'peek-a-boo' with a baby, you will have seen its surprise and delight when your face or the toy reappeared. Why is a baby so surprised by this? Surely, the baby or child must know the toy was still there, just hidden out of sight.

In fact, a young child's experience of the world is so concrete, so built upon its primary senses, that when the toy is hidden, it ceases to exist.

As a child gets older, it explores and begins to create abstract 'maps' of its surroundings. There comes an age when a child is no longer surprised by the reappearing toy, and you will see a different behaviour – when you hide the toy, the child will look for it.

There is a conflict between the data available to the child. Its senses say that the toy no longer exists, but its experience says the toy is just out of sight. The child then takes action to resolve this conflict.

Between 4 and 12 months old, the child has started to call upon its internal map, and is valuing its own internal data above external data.

Many years later, at a magic show, that early surprise and delight is rekindled when the child looks for the coin in the magician's hand, only to find it empty.

The more you expose a child to rich, sensory experiences, the more information it has to build new maps and develop new ways of thinking about the world.

The sensorimotor stage, 0 - 2 years

At this time, the child is developing its sensory awareness and its motor skills. It is learning to sense the world around it and take action in order to meet its needs.

Age	Developmental stage
1-4 months	"Primary circular reactions" - an action, such as thumb sucking, becomes its own stimulus which leads to the same action.
4-12 months	"Secondary circular reactions" - an action, such as squeezing a toy, leads to an external stimulus such as a sound which leads to the same action.
12-24 months	"Tertiary circular reactions" - an action is repeated in different situations, such as hitting different objects to hear the different sounds they make.

Pre-operational stage, 2 - 7 years

At this time, the child develops the ability to use symbols to represent objects and events in the 'real world'.

A symbol is used to represent something, and you can have many different symbols to represent the same thing.

The child develops a sense of past and future at this stage, and the ability to mentally manipulate symbols. This marks the child's progression to the next stage of development, and is what Jean Piaget called the ability to 'decentre', which he investigated with the following experiment, which you can try for yourself with a table, some household objects and a selection of children.

Piaget sat down at a table with a model mountain range on it. He asked a child to tell him which view of the mountain range Piaget could see. Younger children indicated their own point of view, older children indicated Piaget's point of view, demonstrating their ability to see the model from an imaginary angle.

Here is a top view of a version of Piaget's mountain range (two balls and a cube) showing the positions of Piaget and a child.

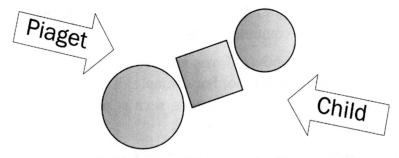

Which of the following views would the child see, and which would Piaget see?

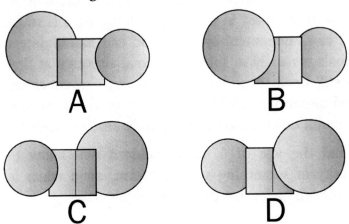

Learning by talking

One of the most important abstract maps that a child learns to use is that of language. Language is a symbolic representation of the world, in that the word 'apple' is not an apple, it is a symbol that represents an apple. When the child learns to use the symbol, it can communicate its needs to a parent or carer.

Children learn to use many different types of symbol in order to communicate their needs, and parents have differing levels of success in interpreting those symbols.

Games such as charades are good ways to teach children to use different communication symbols.

At around 18 months old, you will see a child develop the use of other symbols too. For example, it will use objects as toys to represent other objects, such as play food or toy villages with cars and people.

Concrete operations stage, 7 - 11 years

The word 'operations' refers to logical calculations or rules that are used in solving problems. At this stage, the child can understand symbols and can manipulate those symbols mentally to solve problems, although at first this will still need to be within the context of concrete, real world situations. Children learning maths at school still work with objects rather than purely abstract ideas.

Around the age of 6, most children will know that a quantity of something stays constant, even when it is a different shape or in a different container.

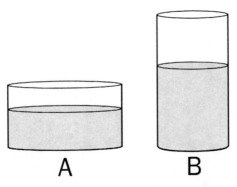

A   B

Prior to this stage, a child will tend to see glass B as being the most full because the level of liquid in it is higher, when in fact both have the same amount of liquid in, which a child at this stage will understand. The amount of liquid is 'conserved' regardless of how it is stored.

Having said that, many adults are similarly fooled by the shape of a glass, much to the joy of the owners of bars and restaurants who use glasses and other presentation methods to trick us into thinking that we're getting more for our money.

Formal operations stage, 12+ years

At this point, the child is developing adult thinking abilities, particularly the ability to use logical and abstract operations and form theories about how things work.

When you appreciate how the mind develops, you'll begin to see how learning is a process which can be studied and copied. Regardless of our age, job or social status, we all have, quite literally, a lifetime of experience to share with each other.

[6]Learning

Before we get into modelling, it's important to understand something about learning, because this is the natural process that we are trying to unpick and replicate through modelling. By understanding the learning process, you'll find it easier to implement the models that you create with the help of this book.

While a craftsman spends a lifetime mastering his craft, it needn't take a lifetime to master a specific skill within that craft. Much of the learning time is redundant; practising motor actions instead of learning decision criteria, or performing tasks which have no bearing on the particular skill that we want to model.

Whilst there are many theories about learning, representing the different ways that you can analyse the subject, the one I'd like to briefly discuss here is Kolb's theory because it relates to a cyclical learning process rather than a static learning preference or style.

David Kolb published his learning styles model in 1984 as Kolb's experiential learning theory (ELT). It divides the learning cycle into four stages, as follows.

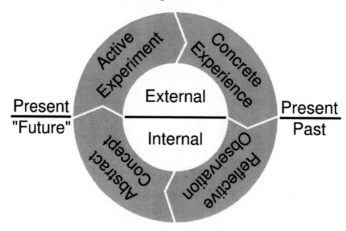

Concrete Experience

This stage is one of real, physical, direct, first hand, visceral sensory experience. An experience might comprise any combination of sights, sounds, feelings, tastes or smells and in fact, you may know that all experiences and therefore all memories comprise all of these elements, even though some of them may be less prominent than others. A concrete experience is external to us and therefore always in the present.

Reflective Observation

Once we've had a concrete experience, we reflect on it. We cast our mind back, both consciously and unconsciously, and relive the experience so that we can make generalisations and draw conclusions. Research has shown that the structure within the brain known as the hippocampus creates a kind of 'action replay' of emotionally charged events, etching them forever in our long term memories. Reflective observation is internal to us and therefore always in the past, and the observation isn't necessarily visual, it features all of the sensory information which was present in the original experience.

Abstract Concept

Having relived the experience, we take those generalisations and conclusions and use them to create an abstract concept, a set of rules or principles which govern the experience and others like it. When abstract conceptualisation involves mental rehearsal, it is internal and appears to be in the future, when in fact it is a replay of the past as we cannot internally represent the future; it doesn't yet exist.

Active Experiment

Finally, we take the abstract concept and test it by applying it to new situations. A child tests a range of household objects to find out if they float as well as his lost balloon. A father gives all of the house plants a close shave in order to 'try out' the new hedge trimmer that he received for his birthday. Active experimentation leads full circle to a new concrete experience which either affirms or contradicts the abstract concept. Active experimentation is always external and in the present.

Honey and Mumford

Onto Kolb's four learning stages, Peter Honey and Alan Mumford later mapped the four roles shown in the diagram; Activist, Pragmatist, Theorist and Reflector. In Kolb's model, there are four learning stages which we might paraphrase as Think, Do, Feel and Watch.

Activist

Activists need to do something and they learn by experimenting. They need to experience something for themselves and work out how they feel about it, so they make decisions based on their instincts more than on logic. Activists seek hands on experience and get bored with implementation.

Activists say, "Can I have a go?"

Pragmatist

Pragmatists like to do what works. They like to know what works in the real world. Pragmatists like to find practical applications for ideas.

Pragmatists say, "Does it work?"

Theorist

Theorists like to observe what's going on and then form a theory or opinion about it. Theorists like evidence, logical explanations, abstract models, facts and figures. They don't like subjectivity and exaggeration.

Theorists say, "How does it work?"

Reflector

Reflectors like to observe and reflect and turn things around from different points of view. They like to use their imagination to solve problems rather than diving in like the activists. They like to take time to ponder and don't rush into decisions until they think that they have covered all the angles.

Reflectors say, "Let me think about it."

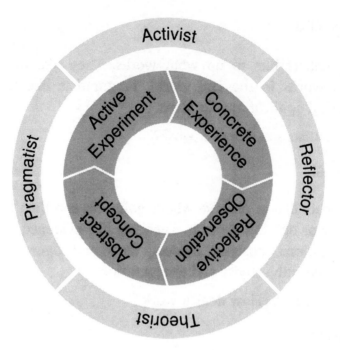

People are not fixed in these roles, they are preferences. We all need time to reflect, we all need to take part, we all need to create rules and we all need experience to confirm those rules. You could therefore think of the roles above as a bias towards a particular learning sequence or a tendency to spend longer in one part of the learning cycle.

You might even consider that the learning style is the point in the cycle at which a person prefers to begin, however a complete learning experience must always involve the full cycle because that reflects how our life experiences are formed. Life happens, we ponder on it, we wonder what it all means and then figure out what to do about it. We probably don't have a great deal of control over life as a learning experience which happens whether we like it or not, but Kolb's work gives us a language and a framework for understanding what happens when as person *intentionally sets out to learn something new*.

This probably calls to mind the idea of 'conscious incompetence'. When I know that I don't know something, I set out to learn it. I know that I want to record my favourite TV show, but I can't for the life of me remember how to program the video recorder.

However, when learning is not motivated by the individual, the idea of 'unconscious incompetence' is more relevant. I have no idea that there are such things as superconductors, or cytoblasts, or actuaries, and that's generally because I had no interest in them. Should I become interested, just because someone else thinks that it's important for me to know about such things?

Learning theories are important because the primary aim of modelling is to produce a model which can be replicated. In order to 'install' a model in someone else, you'll need to understand how they learn.

Some proponents of NLP would have you believe that a model can be installed in a matter of seconds, but this is unrealistic. Studies of brain plasticity and learning show that a realistic time to master a new behaviour is about six months, with daily activity, reflection and integration. It's interesting that the most current and advanced work in neuroscience adds weight to what teachers have said for generations; that students need regular practice over a prolonged period of time together with proper rest in order to truly master a new skill. A good night's sleep really is part of the learning process.

A common approach to learning is to structure a sequence of activities as follows:

1. Present a theory

2. Find practical examples of the theory

3. Use the theory to build a personal concept

4. Apply that personal concept

5. Reflect on the experience to construct a new theory

6. Repeat the whole process with a new and perhaps contradictory theory

A psychology student might learn about Jung's theory of archetypes, looking at the descriptions and finding real examples of people who fit those descriptions. They might use a type indicator tool or psychometric instrument to bring their own personal experience into the learning process. They would then work out how they could apply the theory in their own work and practically try it out, perhaps using Jungian archetypes as a set of signposts for a coaching intervention. After spending some time working with this, they would reflect on what they had learned about the theory, its practical application and about their own preconceptions and experiences, abstracting those experiences and creating a new theoretical model.

The whole process can be repeated, and if that is done with a contradictory theory, the student will greatly open up their thinking on the subject and develop a richer, deeper understanding of it.

The ability to truly understand apparently contradictory explanations is the very basis of intellect and of science.

To be able to explain the motion of the planets around the sun and, at the same time, to be open to the possibility that the sun comes up because sufficient sacrifices have been made to the Sun God is the basis of the scientific method; to reject no idea, no matter how incredible, and to test every theory, no matter how obvious.

The saying, "the exception proves the rule" is generally used to mean that an exception makes the rule correct:

"I'm always on time!"

"You were late this morning!"

"Well, the exception proves the rule..."

However, the origin of the word "prove" doesn't mean 'confirm', it means 'test'. The phrase actually means, "the exception tests the rule", which makes absolute sense.

Theoretical models can never, ever be 'true' or 'right' and your mindset must always be one of curiosity, of testing in order to prove the rule.

The approach to modelling that I am detailing in this book is not a replacement for a thorough learning process. If anything, it is a foundation for the instructional design process, where you can use a high performance model as the basis for the design of a learning intervention.

As you will see later, modelling is as much about transferring culture as it is about transferring specific behavioural skills.

⁷Modelling

A large part of the approach that we'll be taking in modelling excellence is based on the original techniques of Neuro-Linguistic Programming.

Before NLP became a hyped up self help industry, it was a system created by Richard Bandler and John Grinder for coding the internal thought processes and sequences of a particular innate skill.

Bandler was a mathematics student and Grinder an assistant linguistics professor. Their work in modelling the linguistic patterns of notable therapists led to their theory that excellent communicators do not behave randomly; their language and behaviour are highly organised on multiple levels. The notation that they developed for mapping sequences of thought processes was first published in books such as Patterns of the Hypnotic Techniques of Milton H. Erickson, Volumes I & II and Structure of Magic, Volumes I and II.

The techniques of NLP which are taught at Practitioner level are the result of modelling the intuitive skills of people such as Milton H Erickson, Fritz Perlz and Virginia Satir.

Therefore, the Practitioner techniques are not NLP in themselves - they are the results of NLP.

Many people confuse NLP with its techniques - including many of its trainers.

This is like saying that art is just oil painting, or architecture is just building skyscrapers. The tools you will learn on a course, or read about in a book, are the results of NLP - they do not define NLP itself. A good NLP Practitioner will go on to model excellence in other people and create new tools in new situations. Someone who has not embraced this spirit of modelling excellence will use the tools in a prescriptive, inflexible way and - guess what? - sometimes they will work and sometimes they wont. People with the flexibility to model excellence and create new tools just keep on going until the problem is solved, and usually it doesn't look like they're doing anything at all.

In order to understand and apply NLP effectively, you really do need to understand the concept of modelling. People who just take NLP as its techniques find that those techniques work some of the time. By modelling the problem first, you'll find that the techniques work first time, every time.

If we take the fast phobia cure as an example, if you use it with ten people who have a phobia, you might find it works with half of them. This doesn't mean that the technique is only effective 50% of the time - it means that half of the people you used it with did not have a phobia. A common example is 'fear of flying'. I'll go out on a limb here and say that no-one is afraid of flying. There are, however, a lot of people who are afraid of crashing. There is no point doing a fast phobia cure on something like this because it is not a phobic response. A fear of crashing takes a great deal of imagination, and so the first step is to find out how the problem works by modelling it so that you can choose or create an appropriate technique.

NLP training was originally aimed at experienced therapists, as you will discover in Frogs into Princes. The aim was to give them a new set of tools to add to their existing professional knowledge, which is very different to delivering training to people with little or no experience in psychology or therapy. In some ways, NLP has become attached to the life coaching industry and suffers the same superficial, 'quick fix' criticisms.

NLP techniques can be regarded as simple recipes for personal problem solving. If someone has a phobia, use the Fast Phobia Cure, if they are stuck in a restrictive pattern of behaviour, use the Six Step Reframe. There is nothing wrong with them as simple recipes, but a good chef is never limited by a recipe book.

In the world of electronics, there are good engineers and there are average engineers. The average engineers will fix a problem by replacing all the components until they find the one that was causing the problem. A good engineer will locate the problem first before changing the faulty component.

Good engineers (in fact, all good professionals) observe behaviour. They know how something behaves when it is working normally, so they know where to start looking when it does not behave normally. Average engineers do not observe behaviour in the same way.

When I was an engineer, I learned to observe behaviour, because it was the only way to fix complex problems. If you don't know what the equipment does when it's working properly, how can you know what is wrong with it when it isn't working properly?

Psychologists study mental illnesses so that they can learn more about them. Unless you also study people without the illnesses, that information is useless. Schizophrenics, according to Richard Bandler, can't tell the difference between what is real and what is imagined (whatever reality is). Unless we figure out how average people can tell the difference, we can't help the schizophrenics. Whilst Bandler is rather critical of the medical community, you should remember that every trial for a new medical intervention is first tested with control groups, precisely to determine these differences.

If you want to improve the performance of a sales team, it's no use focusing on the under-performers. We need to figure out what the over-performers are doing first. NLP modelling is inherently systemic and ecological. By modelling a successful sales person, we can understand the mindset that works for that team, in that company, in that market, with those products and those customers. Therefore, by teaching that mindset to other sales people in the same team, we have an instantly workable process.

By comparing the high performers to average performers, we are using the well established principle of the 'control group'.

Many people assume that this means the behavioural knowledge required to perform a complex task is locked away and is irretrievable. We get a glimpse of the knowledge through observing behaviour, but there is no way to extract the knowledge itself. Other people went on to guess at the behavioural programming, based on their observations, but they tried to guess 'why' the individual behaved that way instead of asking 'how'. 'Why' is irrelevant. If I want to copy your talent for writing music, or sticking to a diet, or remember people's names at a party, I don't need to know why you do it. I just need to know how, so I can learn to do it. If I decide to acquire this skill for myself, I will have my own, personal, unique "why".

Traditional 'body language' is an example of this, where a particular movement 'means' something specific such as arrogance or fear. Body movement is not a language in itself, it's a component of communication. The effects of 'body language' training are still with us today, lingering on in presentation skills courses that teach people how to stand so that they look confident. Isn't it better just to be confident, and let your body naturally communicate that?

We can say with some certainty that we just don't understand how the brain works, because there are many competing schools of thought. Behaviourists say that we can only observe behaviour, therefore whatever goes on inside is unknowable and therefore irrelevant. This philosophy leads us to the conclusion that other people might be zombies with no internal consciousness at all, and we would be unable to determine the difference.

Existentialists argue that we create our own experience and therefore we can only observe and think subjectively. There is no objectivity, and the human observer can never be removed from what is being observed. An apple is only red in relation to its human observer and a falling tree only makes a sound in the forest when an illegal logger cuts it down with his noisy chainsaw.

The originators of NLP, John Grinder and Richard Bandler, were first interested in excellent communicators in the field of personal change, so they went to talk to some of the most respected and innovative therapists at the time. They found that these people had certain things in common to do with they way that they communicated.

By exploring these similarities, a model was developed of the way these people used language to influence patterns of thought and behaviour.

Techniques such as anchoring and reframing are applications of NLP. NLP itself is the process by which we extracted those techniques from the minds of real people.

NLP is therefore not a therapeutic technique in itself; it is just a coincidence that NLP was first used to model therapists, and Bandler and Grinder probably saw that as a worthwhile market to offer training in. However, other people have since used the same basic toolkit to model excellence in business, sport, the performing arts, education and many other disciplines.

Modelling with NLP is as much a mindset of curiosity as an explicit set of tools. This mindset will help you to learn interesting things from experts, from people you admire and from yourself. It is an open mindedness, in which you suspend any questions about why someone is doing something and instead only observe how they are doing something. This initial observation is then followed up with detailed questions about *how they decided* what to do at each stage of the process.

For example, driving a car is a very complex set of behaviours which take many months to learn and years to thoroughly master. Yet the individual actions that a driver takes aren't new. A child can imitate the actions of a racing driver, but can they drive a car? Generally, no, but not because they don't know how to steer or operate the controls, but because they don't know *how* to steer and *when* to operate *which* controls.

When you watch your colleagues, clients and friends, you will notice that they do certain things in a certain order. You will be able to watch the process by which they individually behave in order to achieve their goals.

There seem to be a number of hallmarks of a talent:

- The person is able to get consistent results without having to think about the process or even being aware of it

- When asked, the person is a little surprised that the skill is worth modelling. They will often deny they are good at the task and will be surprised that everyone doesn't do it.

- When you first ask, "how do you do it?" they answer, "I don't know - I just do it"

The mechanic movements of driving a car are easy to master. You can observe your parent or driving instructor and you can copy the movements required to press a pedal or change gear. But how did they know when to change gear? How did they know which gear to turn into? How did they know how hard and for how long to depress the pedal? These are the internal decision processes that distinguish an average driver from a talented one. For most of us, this may not make a lot of difference, but for a racing driver, microseconds of efficiency at the decision level lead to the difference between starting out in pole position and ending up in the pits.

One of the other important aspects of NLP modelling is that we model what is working rather than trying to classify what isn't working. Rather than researching people who have phobias, we look for people who used to have phobias but now don't and we figure out what they did to get rid of their phobias. Many NLP trainers - and at least half of NLP's creators - are highly critical of the therapeutic and pyschological community for researching phobias and other conditions. I'd like to distance myself from their criticism, as I find it to be naïve and uniformed. My view is that studying a phobia as merit and studying the way in which a phobia can change has merit. NLP is not concerned with understanding the nature of the phobia, and for this reason, NLP is often criticised for being a "quick fix" solution. On the other hand, proponents of NLP would ask why anyone would want a "slow fix". In terms of modelling, the skill that we want to extract and teach to others is the skill of losing a phobia. There is generally less value in teaching someone to learn a phobia, although I sometimes think that learning a phobia of cream cakes wouldn't be a bad thing for someone who had trouble dieting.

This brings us to the issue of context. One of NLP's 'presuppositions' states "There is a positive intention motivating every behaviour and a context in which it has value". The presuppositions are the beliefs upon which NLP's techniques are layered. For example, a technique for a tennis serve is built upon a series of beliefs, such as a a belief that you enjoy playing tennis and want to improve your game. If your foundation was a belief that you could never master tennis and your serve would always be weak then your learning process, and therefore your learning outcome, would be subtly different. Maybe not different enough to affect a friendly game in the back garden, but certainly different enough to make the difference between picking up a medal at Wimbledon and picking up litter on Wimbledon Common.

Finally, bear in mind that all of this fits into NLP's view of the world, which is not shared by everyone. For example, where NLP sees a phobia as a learned response, a different school of thought says:

> "A phobia symbolises repressed capabilities. Angst themes that have not been totally worked out with parents are internally split off and projected as childlike parts onto a trigger (e.g. insect, bird and animal phobias). Apart from that, triggering events are not only moments of fright, but often situations of loss, This points to other relationship issues that indirectly show up as secondary gains."
>
> NLP Ecology Redefined
> Annegret Hallanzy

Whether you believe that or not is up to you. I'm merely asking you to regard all of this with a dose of perspective.

Perhaps the most important distinction here is that other schools of thought see something like a phobia as being rooted in the past and therefore difficult to change, whereas NLP sees a phobia as being learned in the past yet replayed in the present, making it easy to change.

We could perhaps compare it to something like a book versus a document on your computer. A book was written and printed in the past and is fixed. You can write on it, highlight text, but you cannot fundamentally edit it. If you cut some text out, a gap remains. A document on your computer can be edited any time you like and it will reformat seamlessly around the changes.

I don't know which is 'true', and I don't suppose there will ever be a universal agreement until we can talk to whoever designed us, but since there is some debate on who that is, there can be no single point of view. Make up your own mind despite what anyone else says, unless someone else is saying make up your own mind in which case just do what they tell you to.

We are models

In the article 'Mirror Neurons and the Simulation Theory of Mind Reading', Gallese and Goldman evaluate evidence for our ability to infer others' internal emotional states as well as the processes behind their behaviour. They put forward the idea that we developed this ability in order to learn behaviours, and that this ability now gives us empathy and the ability to predict others' behaviour.

A map is a model. It is not the same as the place that it represents, but it helps you to condense a representation of that place onto a single sheet of paper so that you can find your way around.

Our ability to construct abstract models of the outside world means that we are ourselves models of reality. Knowing that $2+2=4$ is not the same as having 4 apples, and we understand both how to create abstract models as well as how to apply them to real life situations.

A thought about a thing is not the same as the thing itself. The model is not reality. The map is not the territory.

Consider the model of sensory filtering that is presented in NLP and other schools of thought, and consider how it guides our own learning processes.

Finally, remember the NLP presupposition:

All distinctions human beings are able to make concerning our environment and our behaviour can be usefully represented through the visual, auditory, kinaesthetic, olfactory, and gustatory senses

Recognising Models

Let's start our modelling journey with a deceptively simple exercise. It's important to begin by understanding the distinction between a thing and a model of that thing, because we generally use language interchangeably in this respect. A colleague might point at some pixels on a computer screen and say, "The report's here, but I can't find the supporting spreadsheet for it". In the Steve Martin film 'The Man with Two Brains', a journalist asks about the doctor's wife, points to a doll and asks, "Is that her?" The doctor replies, "No. That's just a statue of her."

If you look around you, you'll see models as well as models of models. You'll also see people interacting with models as if they are interacting with the real thing. Is it that they can't tell the difference? Not necessarily. It's more likely to be a demonstration of our remarkable ability to interact with abstract concepts *as if* we are interacting with real, concrete concepts, a sign of reaching the developmental stage of symbolic operations, mentioned earlier. We use a map as if it really is the territory.

Can you recognise the models that are all around you?

7.1 Every model is a generalisation

In order to simplify an experience into a model, we have to delete some of it and distort the rest so that it can be generalised into a simple concept or representation.

List as many types of model aeroplane as you can. I don't mean Spitfire, Lancaster, Tornado etc., they might all be 'Airfix kits'. You need to list other types of model, only in the left hand column:

Type of model	
Airfix kits	

What examples of model aeroplanes did you come up with? Here are a few suggestions for you to compare with your own list:

- A paper aeroplane
- A computer simulation of airflow over a wing
- A wind tunnel model
- A bronze statue of an aeroplane
- A Hollywood film set
- The phrase "Boeing 747"
- A flight simulator
- A fire training simulator
- The word "aeroplane"
- The sound of an aeroplane
- A CAD drawing used to build an aeroplane
- The image that comes to mind when you think of an aeroplane

7.2 Every model has a purpose

In the right hand column of the table in exercise 5.1, write the purpose of the models that you have listed.

Every model is generalised from the original, and that process of generalisation is guided by the model's purpose. For example, the purpose of an Airfix model is to physically represent the real item but on a smaller scale and to be easy for someone to assemble themselves at home. Therefore, some of the physical details of the real aircraft are missed out because the plastic moulding process cannot reproduce them, and the model itself is made of a material which the real aircraft is not made from.

Every model has a purpose. Every model is functional.

For example, if we list some models of a television set, we might have a circuit diagram, a dolls house model and one of those fake televisions that you find in show homes.

Each has its own purpose.

The dolls house model does not have the same level of detail in its surface appearance as the original, and the circuit diagram tells you nothing about how the television looks. The show home television looks like any television, but none in particular. Its features are generalised so that it does not endorse a particular manufacturer or infringe any registered design features.

Even the word 'television' is itself a model of a television, generalised for communicating the concept and experience of a television to another human being.

The purpose of a model tells us how the original object or event has been condensed into a format suitable for human experience.

Remember that we are generalising objects and events in the outside world, so the first level of filtering is that we are unable to sense much of the information that is available and our perception imposes qualities on an object that are not inherent in it.

You are no doubt aware of the example of colour. This paper is not white. The combination of frequencies of electromagnetic radiation reflecting off the boundary between two regions of matter interfere with cells in your eyes in such a way that your visual perception creates the experience of colour which you have associated with the word 'white'. Because that's such a long winded description of the process, it's easier to say that the paper *is* white, when in fact it isn't. It's also easy to say that the spider *is* scary or the manager *is* mean or the train *is* late, when in fact they are all qualities of our experience, not inherent qualities of the object or event in question.

The word 'is' is a complex equivalence, and a complex equivalence, in meta model, is a generalisation, and in order to generalise, deletions and distortions must first take place, and distortions require internal comparisons in order to know what to distort and how. The whole sequence of events is a complex relationship between external events and internal models of previous events.

NLP modelling

When Bandler and Grinder set out to model the language and behaviour of people such as Milton H Erickson, they did not code directly from their subject. Bandler spent time observing and emulating the subject and Grinder then coded Bandler's behaviour and language.

This process took many months, and from this they created the set of NLP Practitioner techniques. I'm asking you to model very specific skills, and for this you can model directly from the subject.

The process of emulating an entire person's behaviour without attempting to organise or code it is called, in NLP, 'unconscious uptake'. The approach is simple - just copy everything that the subject does and see if you can get the same results. Trying to make sense of their behaviour at this stage narrows your focus and you could easily miss what turns out to be the most important thing.

In Derren Brown's[1] TV series, 'Mind Control', he gets the cashiers at a dog racing track to pay out on losing tickets. When I show this video to people and ask them to work out how he does it, they focus on language patterns, embedded commands, his hand gestures etc. They are trying to organise and code his behaviour at the same time as taking in the whole sequence, and so they inevitably miss the overall structure of the interaction between Derren Brown and the cashier.

---

1   Derren Brown is a British entertainer and 'mentalist' who performs psychological magic such as getting ordinary people to conduct armed robberies or confess to a murder that never happened.

If you model a high performing sales person, you might notice that they say, "do you know what I mean?", they drive a Ford Mondeo and they eat ham sandwiches for lunch. You might rule out these things because they obviously have nothing to do with sales performance. The NLP modelling approach aims, where possible, to rule out nothing until you can reliably replicate their results.

I conducted a modelling project for a UK retailer where their HR team identified high performers in three roles and asked me to investigate how these people were consistently outperforming their peers, both in 'hard' measurements and in more subjective criteria.

In each case, the high performers turned out to be exhibiting different skills than those predicted by the HR team. The unique combination of their attitude, behaviour and the cultural environment of the retailer resulted in their results matching the retailer's criteria for high performance. Whilst their skills may be broadly similar to those of their peers in other retailers, there are sufficient cultural differences for this to make the difference between average and high performance.

For example, the HR team believed that coaching skills were vital for a good manager, so they had invested in a training program. The average store managers certainly spent time coaching their staff, but the high performers spent no time at all coaching staff.

The relevance of this to modelling in NLP is that purists such as John Grinder advocate that 'unconscious uptake' is a vital part of the process, whereas my opinion is that this was vital for them in the creation of NLP because they were starting with a very broad set of performance criteria - they couldn't tell what people like Erickson and Satir were doing differently.

Where you are modelling a very specific behaviour and you have full access to multiple role models and objective performance measurements, it can be easier to bypass this step, go directly to coding and instead select the critical elements of the model by cross referencing and comparing high performers to average performers. This is very similar to Dilts' Success Factor Modelling approach.

The reason for choosing average performers to compare to rather than poor performers is that it is important to keep the intended outcome consistent. It is also vital that you use external criteria as the reference point for high performance. Poor performers are too far away from the average to be a valuable comparison, and in fact what we really want to ascertain is what the high performers do differently to the average person. The lowest performers are equally different to the average, but in the wrong direction.

If you model athletes, the high performers are the ones who run the fastest. In the retailer mentioned above, the high performing store managers had the highest sales figures and the lowest wastage figures. Put them in a different retailer and their performance will be different because the cultural environment is different.

If you have already looked up 'Derren Brown dog racing' on YouTube, you might be wondering how he does it. He approaches the betting window with a losing ticket, hands it over and confidently says, "This is a winning ticket". The cashier puts the ticket into the automated reader, looks confused and says, "I'm sorry, this hasn't won"

Derren bangs on the wall and says, mysteriously, "This is the dog you're looking **for**. That's why we came to this **win**dow." The cashier apologises and pays out.

"Aha!", you cry. It's obvious. The winning dog was number four, "for" is therefore an ambiguity that the cashier interprets as the winning number, and the stress on the syllable "win" is an embedded command which the cashier is unable to resist. It's a nice theory.

However, step back and look at the big picture. What is the cashier's job? Is it to determine if bets have been won or lost? No, the cashier's job is to take bets and then to pay out on winning bets. Why would anyone approach the window with a losing bet? The job is fairly monotonous, the interactions with customers minimal and the routine is check ticket, pay out, check ticket, pay out, check ticket.... and so on.

It makes more sense to pay out than not, so the cashier does what we all do when facing conflict; she overrules the one piece of information which doesn't fit the norm; the small detail that the ticket is for a loser.

Meta Model

Meta Model, literally a model of models, is a way of interpreting language as a symbolic model of the internal representation of a person's experience.

A person experiences reality and generalises it into their internal model of the world. By regarding the structure of this model as significant in itself, we can determine the means by which that person creates that model.

My father still has the A to Z road map of Birmingham and the road map of Great Britain that he had when I was a child. They don't have any of the roads that have been built in the past 40 years on them, and some entire towns are missing too!

A model being out of step with reality doesn't make it wrong, it simply represents a different reality. When that reality, or more accurately the 'reality map' no longer reflects the reality shared by the majority of other people, no amount of organised behaviour will ever bring the 'desire map' towards the 'reality map' because the reality map is so inaccurate.

Therefore, Meta Model can recover the information lost when our perceptions are encoded into our world model, enabling us to update that model and function more effectively. By effective, I mean that our chosen actions are more likely to get the results we want because the model that those actions are based on is sufficiently useful that our actions have a similar result in 'real life'.

In coaching, we talk about the importance of the 'first minute'; the time at the very beginning of a coaching session when the client is communicating their unconscious and conscious desires and experiences. You could consider the 'first minute' to be the time when the current model is being 'loaded' and represented without judgement or distortion, hence the similarity between the unconscious representation and the external communication which enables us to deduce the structure of the model (problem etc.) very quickly, if we are paying attention. In reality, a minute is far too long, and if you are trying to pay attention to all of the person's communication for this length of time, you will most likely have missed the structure, which is usually played out before they begin to speak.

For example, on a NLP Practitioner course, I asked for someone to help me demonstrate this principle. A student volunteered, walked towards the chair at the front of the room, stopped half way, returned to his chair to have a drink of water and then came to the front. When I asked him what behaviour he'd like to use as an example, he said that he often starts projects but hesitates before he starts, goes back to make sure he's doing the right thing and ends up feeling unproductive. What he said about a generic work situation mirrored his behaviour in joining me at the front of the room.

By paying attention to what the client does *before they think you have started*, you will gather all of the information you need in order to effect change.

Personally, this never ceases to amaze me. By observing someone carefully before they 'begin', you can actually stop them mid sentence, tell them the exact nature of their 'problem' and effect a solution, without them telling you anything about it, or so they think. In fact, they had been screaming the information at you from the moment you first saw them.

Being able to model a client's reality and mental processes at Master Practitioner level requires a thorough understanding of the Meta Model. Sadly, at Practitioner level, most trainers gloss over the Meta Model as if it's a collection of coaching questions which may or may not be useful. In fact, the Meta Model is the foundation of NLP, from which all techniques can be recreated. When you can use the Meta Model, you can model the sequence of events that took someone from being afraid of dogs to being comfortable with them, or from being afraid of picking up the telephone to make sales calls to finding it a relatively easy part of their job. When you have modelled those sequences, you can create techniques that you can then apply to help other people in a similar predicament.

The Meta Model is covered extensively in The NLP Practitioner Manual[2] but I have included it here in summary in a later chapter because it is so vitally important. When you understand the Meta Model, modelling really will "fall into place" and you will be able to amaze your clients and colleagues by telling them all about their "problem" when they don't think they have told you anything about it. As a coaching tool alone, it is invaluable for getting inside the client's world and I can't encourage you enough to learn it thoroughly.

Mind you, if you do now go and learn it thoroughly, then I obviously *have* encouraged you enough, thereby proving myself wrong.

---

2   CGW Publishing, ISBN 978-1-9082930-3-9, Freeth & Smith

Isomorphism

Literally, a similarity in shape. The structure of a person's language is the same as the structure of their experience and perceptions. Their language and their behaviour are isomorphic. The structure of one gives us the structure, and the ability to predict and influence, the other.

An oak tree and the human brain are isomorphic, in that the physical appearance and function of the tree's branches and the brain's blood vessels follow similar mathematical rules for their growth and therefore look alike.

The phrase, "Let's hit the shops" could have a structural similarity to the way in which someone approaches a shopping trip, and afterwards, they might quite literally feel, "wiped out".

Taking language literally is probably the single most valuable skill in learning and applying the meta model effectively. Treating metaphors as if they are literal descriptions of an internal experience is usually far more productive than pushing the person to abandon their metaphors and give you a detailed analysis of their experience. For example, when someone feels deflated, or pushed from pillar to post, or like a kid in a sweet shop, they are using metaphorical language to convey a very literal experience. I suppose the rule of thumb is that all language is metaphorical, in that a word is not the same as the thing it represents. Since all language is a representation, we are potentially talking about two different types of representation; a more literal one where the person is choosing their words perhaps carefully, and a more metaphorical one, where the person's unconscious mind has more of an input into the language chosen, revealing the unconscious thought processes that drive the behaviour in question.

In coaching, I find it personally useful to visualise the forces acting upon a person as indicated in their language. For example, frustration combines a force or desire acting upon an immovable barrier. When you absorb yourself in the client's language, it is easy to accept the constants of the situation; that they cannot move the barrier, that they must achieve their goal and so on. Yet, when you visualise frustration as a force acting against a barrier, it is easy to see some potential solutions:

- Move the barrier
- Go round, over or under the barrier
- Apply the force in the opposite direction
- Stop applying the force
- Have someone help you
- Stand on the other side of the barrier and pull
- Recognise the barrier as a *safety* barrier
- Notice that the barrier has gaps in it
- Send information over the barrier instead of trying to physically move past it
- Recognise that it is actually the belief in a need for force which created the barrier in the first place

A director of a public sector organisation recently told me about some organisational problems. Six years after a merger with another organisation, they two were no more integrated than they were before the merger. The executive team were highly educated and, on paper, had the right capabilities. Yet what they had actually created was a divide, a barrier between themselves and their managers. A barrier stops you getting out, but it also stops nasty things getting in, and, the executives had protected themselves against bad news.

In the space of one three minute conversation, the director twice used the phrase "go around it" as a metaphor for "solve the problem".

What does that metaphor say to you? Does it suggest that the problem is something that the executives are ready to tackle and resolve once and for all? Or do you think they're still trying to avoid it?

Until the executives stop trying to go round the problem, they won't succeed. Why? Because there is no problem to go around. The 'problem' is a metaphor for their behaviour. How can they go around their own behaviour?

As a course of action, this metaphor alone tells us that the executives need to accept responsibility for their own behaviour and results before any changes can be made. It also tells us that they are very sensitive about the issue, and we have to tread very carefully.

Just taking a moment to think about metaphors in literal terms is probably the single biggest time saver for anyone involved in problem solving of any kind.

Strategies and the TOTE model

The ability to change the process by which we experience reality is more often valuable than changing the content of our experience of reality

A strategy is a specific sequence of steps that are necessary to perform a particular task.

Crucially, a strategy is NOT a behaviour. You cannot say that you have a strategy for cooking pasta to perfection. It's a program, at best, and if there is any conscious thought involved at all then it's not even that.

Strategies are by definition unconscious, therefore they are decision making processes that take place before you are consciously aware of an external stimulus. In fact, your moment of awareness often coincides with the output of the strategy. For example, if you are afraid of spiders then your strategy has finished long before you are aware that there is a spider in the room. The strategy is the decision making process, and when we are modelling talented people, it is their decisions that we must value most.

Pretty much any idiot can copy a behaviour. The key that marks out the difference between average and exemplary performance is the ability to make decisions that govern that behaviour.

Driving a car comprises a very simple set of behaviours. You wave your hands up and down, you do something akin to stirring a pudding and you move your feet up and down. But knowing when to do these things, and how much to do them, is the key to being able to drive and just 'going through the motions'. When you first started learning to drive, going through the motions is exactly what you did. You made no decisions about where to go, how fast to get there, when to start, when to stop, when to turn and so on. All you could manage was to operate the controls of the car. Anything else was way above your level of competency. As you began to master the mechanical movements that cause the car to respond to your commands, you could relax a little and concentrate on the outside world. Whoa! There are other cars out there! And people! And stray dogs! The roads are a dangerous place, and you had to learn how to navigate the many obstacles that appear before you. The majority of this learning process isn't mechanical, it's purely mental. However, we can't see people doing the mental stuff, so we assume that driving, or playing football, or Tai Chi are physical skills when in fact the physical movements are merely manifestations of a far more complex mental process.

A strategy, then, is a habitual decision that results in a certain course of action based on a certain sensory stimulus.

For example, a skill for goal setting might comprise:

1. Visual construct of desired outcome

2. Kinaesthetic check for congruence of outcome

3. Visual recall of current situation

4. Visual construct of steps required to reach outcome

5. Kinaesthetic check for congruence of outcome

In other words, the person imagines what they would like to have, feels good about it, imagines the steps they need to take and, if it feels right, they do it.

TOTE is a concept developed in 1960 as an extension to the Stimulus Response theories of people such as Pavlov. It simply means that you have a way of knowing to start doing something, a way of knowing to keep doing it and a way to know to stop doing it, and then you can stop thinking about it.

The TOTE model adds an extra layer of formality to the basic strategy in that it adds criteria for starting the strategy and ending it. TOTE stands for Test Operate Test Exit, so to the above example it adds "how do you know when you want something?" and "how do you know when you've got it?" The 'TOTE' is essentially the start and stop for the strategy. You know to shake hands when you meet someone and see their outstretched hand, and you know to stop when you have finished the handshake. You can observe different strategies in operation when the other person wants to hold on for longer than you do, or your hands don't quite connect properly. You may even have experienced shaking hands with someone who didn't intend to shake your hand!

You will typically find that your subject has very specific criteria for the Test and Exit stages, for example someone who is scared of public speaking may know to get scared if there are more than 3 people in the audience. If there are fewer than 3, it doesn't count as a presentation so the 'get scared' strategy doesn't run (the Operate part). This in itself is a very useful change tool - shifting the criteria so that the problem strategy no longer runs. By approaching change work in this way, you are acknowledging the value of the behaviour, the strategy, and simply changing the situation in which it is generated.

In the original NLP model described in books such as 'Structure of Magic' (volumes 1 and 2) and 'Patterns of the Hypnotic Techniques of Milton H Erickson MD' (volumes 1 and 2), you will find many examples and transcripts of strategy elicitations in a therapeutic context.

To make it easier to write a strategy down as a person is speaking, we can use a notation for the steps, as follows:

V	Visual	I	Internal
At	Auditory Tonal	E	External
Ad	Auditory Digital i.e. Language	C	Constructed
K	Kinaesthetic	R	Recalled
O	Olfactory		
G	Gustatory		

In keeping with NLP's model of behaviour being based on the subjective deletions, distortions and generalisations which constitute 'reality', all steps of a strategy are sensory components - modalities - and they can be generated either internally or externally.

For example, Visual Internal, VI, denotes a 'mental image', which could be recalled, such as an image of a recent night out, or it could be constructed, such as an image of you on a future night out.

Clearly, external stimuli are in real time and are neither constructed nor recalled. This presents an important distinction for understanding metaprograms, specifically the idea that all metaprograms are context specific results of an internal or external focus of attention..

Here's a strategy written with the above notation:

Ve > ViR > AdiC > Ki

To indicate a strategy where the person sees something in the outside world, then remembers seeing something, then hears some internal dialogue and finally has a feeling about that - a judgement or conclusion.

The Exit of a strategy - the conclusion - is very often an internal feeling. You'll hear people describe this when they say that a decision feels right, or that they have a gut feeling about something, or that they had a feeling that something was right or wrong.

For example, I might see something in a shop, remember one that I have at home, say to myself, "I could do with a new one of those" and finally feel a desire to buy it. The same overall structure could equally apply to me seeing an apple, comparing it to an internal representation of an apple, saying to myself, "This looks like a nice apple" and feeling a desire to eat it. I could also see someone's face, compare it to a time when that person was angry, say to myself, "Here we go again" and feel a sinking feeling.

For a person, strategies tend to be consistent in multiple contexts. After all, why waste time learning new strategies? Life in general is very conservative and human beings will tend to be consistent, so eliciting a strategy in one context is often valuable in many contexts.

The test of a strategy is only consistency. If a person can get the same result without having to think about it, they are working perfectly and their behaviour is working perfectly because it is achieving what it is meant to. Remember, every behaviour has a positive intention - it is designed to achieve something. Whether that something is good or bad depends only on context.

If we represent a simple TOTE such as shaking hands as a flowchart, this is what we get:

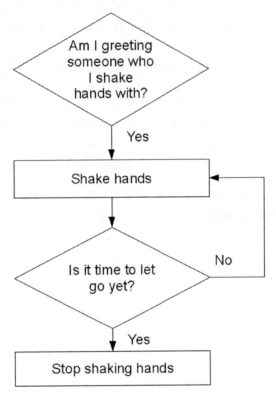

As you can immediately see, we have a problem when representing behavioural decisions in this way. How do you know if this is someone you should shake hands with? Have you met them before? Is it a social situation? Is anyone else shaking hands? Do you have anything sticky on your hands? Are you holding a glass? Are they holding a glass? Do they want to meet you? Once you're shaking hands, how many times do you shake? How long do you hold on for? When do you let go? How do you let go?

Even a very simple behaviour breaks down into so many decision points that to represent it using TOTE flowcharts would be very complicated. In order to make sense of the behaviour, we have to assume so much that the model is generalised beyond comprehension to anyone except someone who already knows how to shake hands.

Whilst you may read about TOTE in NLP, and whilst some trainers use TOTE as a modelling concept, or as a word to describe a skill or behaviour, I would suggest that it complicates things somewhat, because it is too simple.

Let's start with something easier, and which introduces the essential approach to modelling.

7.1 Sequences

Work in pairs for this exercise.

One person describes, for two minutes, a recent experience such as a holiday, night out, party, work situation etc. The other person notes any sensory specific clues that indicate which part of the memory the speaker is recalling at that moment, for example if they are describing an image or playing back someone else's words, or describing feelings or sensations. Just make a note of the sensory system and the clues that give this away, e.g. language, posture, content etc.

	VAKOG	Clues
1		
2		
3		
4		
5		
6		

7		
8		
9		
10		
11		
12		
13		
14		
15		
16		

What did you notice in this exercise?

Are there any patterns in the clues that you picked up?

7.2 Eye Accessing Part 1

Work in pairs for this exercise.

Memorise the question then look your partner right in the eye as you ask it. If you read the question from the notes you will miss the eye accessing which occurs as soon as your partner understands the question - usually about half way through! Make a note of what you observe in the right hand column. You can record in whatever way is easiest for you; arrows, V, A, K etc.

Do not enter into a discussion with your partner at this stage, just ask the questions and record the results.

Where is your bed in relation to the window?	
What's your least favourite colour?	
How does confusion feel?	
Who did you last talk to on the phone?	
How would an anteater sound if it could talk?	
What letter is next to P on a computer keyboard?	
How hard do you have to close your car door?	
When was the last time that you were cosy?	

Is your bathroom hot tap on the right or left?

How does it sound to walk in snow?

What do your bedroom curtains look like?

What is their texture like?

What noise do they make as you open them?

Is your wardrobe door easy or hard to open?

When did you last hear your name?

When were you last in trouble?

What's the 5th word of your favourite song?

What colour clothes were you wearing yesterday?

What colour clothes will you wear tomorrow?

What did your first school smell like?

Which cupboard in your kitchen is the tea in?

The NLP Master Practitioner Manual

In your car, how do you turn the radio on?

What was your first taste of alcohol like?

On a telephone keypad, where is the number 7?

Where was the warmest place you've ever been?

How would you write your name backwards?

What was the last telephone number you dialled?

How does it feel to wade through water?

Which mobile phone ring tone is most irritating?

What time do you think it is? (Without looking!!)

Name one item that is in your fridge

What is your favourite kind of tree?

Eye accessing is a contentious issue in NLP. It's said that, in general, movement to the left infers the recall of an existing memory whilst movement to the right infers the construction of a new experience. This doesn't apply to everyone, and it certainly doesn't mean that someone is lying, just because they're making new pictures in their head. With some people, the left to right accessing is exactly reversed so, once again, it's important to pay attention to the person in front of you, not the generalisation.

If I ask you to recall some visual detail of a memory, such as the colour of a colleague's shirt, you may not remember it right away. You might recall the overall scene, then 'try out' a number of different colours until you feel you've got the right one. This would, for many people, involve a lot of eye accessing up to the right - but you wouldn't be lying.

You will often see a sequence, for example, to recall the sound of walking in snow, you may see your partner look up first, which may indicate they're picturing snow before they can hear it.

Don't be concerned if what you saw your partner doing differs from what you'll find in NLP books; that's quite normal. It is far more important that you observe what actually happens than try to work out what it means.

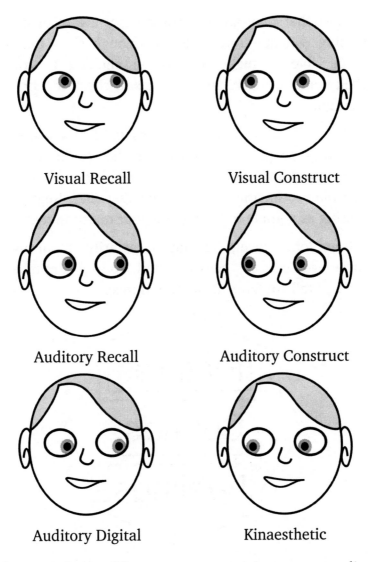

Visual Recall   Visual Construct

Auditory Recall   Auditory Construct

Auditory Digital   Kinaesthetic

It is certainly possible to use eye accessing cues as a direct means to elicit a strategy, and certainly you will see sequences using this method. On one hand, eye accessing sequences are typically very fast, on the other hand, you may see a disagreement between a person's eye accessing and the steps that they verbalise. This is often when a step is so fast that they are not consciously aware of it. Eye accessing will therefore give you enough clues that you will be able to make a start on eliciting a strategy verbally, and will give you a means to check the strategy as you go.

The downside of using eye accessing to elicit a strategy is that many people do not exhibit the 'traditional' eye accessing patterns. You will always need to calibrate first if you plan to incorporate eye accessing cues. Regard eye accessing as a guide to help guide your questioning.

At Practitioner level, it's not necessarily important to analyse eye accessing cues in detail, and for a number of reasons, I tell students to simplify things:

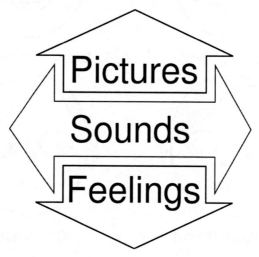

My reasons for simplifying the traditional eye accessing model include:

- The traditional model is fiercely disputed, even within the NLP 'community'

- Not everyone fits the traditional model, therefore it's not sufficiently generalised to be useful

- No recognised research has yet to show any link between eye movements and sensory thoughts

- Perception and cognition are whole brain functions, not localised to a particular area, therefore the traditional NLP neurological model is wildly out of date

- In many people, the left-right orientation of the traditional model is reversed

- The left-right orientation might hold for visual and auditory information, but the model breaks down for kinaesthetic and therefore doesn't fit what we can observe

- Eye accessing is still useful, even though it can't be said to be 'true'

Eye accessing is valuable as part of your modelling toolkit because by observing eye accessing cues, you can make inferences about how someone is thinking and then use that to guide your questioning of them. We may not know why eye accessing cues exist or what they mean, but there is no doubt that they can be consistently observed, and you may find them useful in modelling because they can give clues that reveal underlying processes that your subject finds difficult to articulate.

In this regard, eye accessing cues are no different to any other gesture; they are one more piece of observable evidence that will add consistency to your model.

7.3 Eye Accessing Part 2

Work in pairs for this exercise.

Go back to your notes from the previous exercise. Where you saw more than a simple, single access, find out from your partner what they did in order to answer the question. For example, if you saw, in response to, "How does confusion feel?", a down, up, side, up, down sequence, you might guess that they first tried to access a feeling of confusion, then recalled an image, then heard sounds, then found an appropriate image, then ended back on the feeling.

Work through three examples where you saw more eye movement and discover why you saw a more complex response to the question.

1. Question:
2. Question:
3. Question:

Strategy elicitation

The fundamental technique in NLP modelling is strategy elicitation. If we reduce any behaviour down to a sequence of sensory inputs and motor outputs then that unique sequence is what we call a strategy. Whilst some people refer to this as a meta strategy or a TOTE, we can simply regard a person's vast library of behavioural choices as a nested hierarchy of strategies.

Here's an example of what I mean:

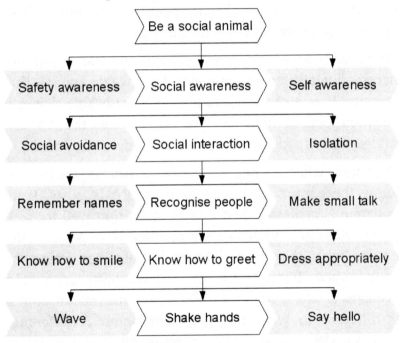

As you can see, in order to execute a strategy, a previous strategy must have executed. We run from one thought to the next, each moment triggering multiple possibilities for our next choice. You have no doubt experienced starting one task, only to be reminded about something else that you need to do and you end up being distracted completely. Every moment leads to the next and builds on what has happened before. The decision to shake someone's hand at a party happens in the blink of an eye, or you could say that the decision happened long ago when you learned to recognise such situations and learned appropriate behaviour.

The lifelong process of learning is feedback based, so you learned that shaking hands resulted in a more enjoyable conversation than punching the other person in the face. If your outcome is to alienate people then your choices and learning experiences will reflect that too.

When you set out to learn something, you might not necessarily have an end in mind. What we do know is that learning is one of the ways in which we bridge that gap between desired state and present state, so that we can bridge that gap more efficiently next time.

Therefore, when we begin to model a strategy, we have to know the context of outcomes in which it exists. If an outcome is achieved then it is by definition well formed. Many NLP Practitioners assume that if a person isn't getting what they want then their outcomes cannot be well formed. Instead, assume that whatever the person achieves is as a result of a well formed outcome, even if it is different to what they say they want. A difference between desire and reality is more often the result of conflicting outcomes rather than a single, ill formed outcome. You will typically observe sequential or simultaneous incongruence in this situation.

We'll come back to incongruence shortly, for now let's work on some strategy elicitation exercises.

7.4 Model a decision strategy

Work in pairs for this exercise. Ask your partner to recall something that they bought recently, which involved a decision.

First, you have to identify the very first point where their decision started; perhaps seeing something in an advert, or feeling that something needed replacing, or hearing someone talk about something, or whatever the first step was for them.

A strategy that serves a specific purpose will be consistent over time, so a decision strategy will likely be the same for any decision. You can probably see how valuable this is in a sales context.

Pin the strategy down to something very specific, otherwise there are too many variables. Focus on the specific decision point, not the whole buying process, and remember that the decision may have been made long before the purchase took place.

Often, you will find that a person has a very fast decision process followed by a longer justification process, so make sure that you focus on the moment the person knew what they wanted.

Test the strategy by playing it back to the subject.

Decision being modelled:

Strategy:

7.5 Model a skill or talent

Work in pairs for this exercise. Ask your partner to identify something that they would call a skill or talent and apply the strategy modelling process as before.

Be very specific about what you are modelling. If they say they are good at time management, that's far too big a set of behaviours for this exercise. You might narrow that down to their ability to choose which of two tasks is the higher priority.

Begin by asking them to tell you about something that they are good at doing and enjoy, and as soon as you hear sequences of representational systems or words such as first or next, you're hearing a strategy. Before that, you will probably hear criteria, and when you do, you can ask, "how do you know...." and that will typically lead you into a strategy.

Test the strategy by playing it back to the subject and trying it out for yourself.

Skill being modelled:

Strategy:

7.6 Model a problem

Work in pairs for this exercise. Ask your partner to identify something that they would call a current problem and apply the strategy modelling process as before.

The key here is to remember that what they describe as a problem is in fact a talent taken out of context, so treat it with the same respect and wonder as for the decision and the talent.

Problem being modelled:

Strategy:

What did you discover from modelling a problem?

What does this mean?

The Meta Model

As promised, I'm going to summarise the Meta Model again because it is vitally important. If you want to learn about it in depth, I recommend that you read the first three books in the recommended reading list at the end of this book. Please bear in mind that for you to be working at Master Practitioner level, you *should* already have a good knowledge of the Meta Model so this chapter is only meant to be a refresher on the subject.

Rather than start with a list of the components of the Meta Model, I'm going to start with three worked examples to show you what is possible. You might then have a useful frame of reference for the summary which follows.[3]

"I've got this situation at work that I just don't know how to handle"

This client is unhappy with a colleague. They would like to slap them in the face or push them off a cliff, but they are keen to find a more socially acceptable solution.

"I get so frustrated that I'm afraid that..."

This father wants to lash out at his child who doesn't behave as the father would like him to, but he knows that's not the best way to solve the problem because he feels angry and afraid about his own father lashing out at him.

---

3   Think back to Kolb's learning styles theory. Which style prefers to start with an example?

"I would like to be better at time management"

Either the client's colleague is more productive and the client is trying to live up to that, or the client has lost motivation and is worried it will affect their career prospects. Either way, they don't really want to be more productive, but they don't want to get into trouble for poor performance either.

How can we deduce these meanings from such brief opening sentences?

Let's work through them using the Meta Model.

"I've got this situation at work that I just don't know how to handle"

In order of priority, I would always suggest tackling nominalisations first. Nominalisations are verbs turned into pseudo-nouns, and they indicate stuck mental processes and will always get in the way of the client's progress. Can you spot the nominalisation in this sentence? It's the word 'situation', which is derived from the verb 'to situate'.

A nominalisation is worth tackling first because in doing so, we achieve two outcomes at once. Firstly, we get the process moving again. Imagine yourself at a meeting. Now imagine yourself meeting someone. What's different? I would guess that the first mental image you made was still, the second moving.

The importance of a still image isn't so much that it is a static moment in time, it is more to do with the future. A still image is a representation "through time", which means that it is *always* true. People who say they are "always in meetings" are speaking correctly, from their distorted point of view. A nominalisation and its associated still image are a prediction of the future, based on a snapshot of the past. In a photograph, the time is always *now*.

The second useful outcome is that a nominalisation, as well as being a generalisation, is a *deletion*, in that the object of the verb is missing.

Subject		Verb		Object
I	was at a	**meeting**		
I		**met**	with	**Fred**

With the object deleted, we only have half of the story. So the word 'situation' is deleting the object; who or what the client situates themselves relative to. A lucky guess makes that a colleague, or perhaps a manager.

The second word to tackle in this statement is 'how'. When you want to go somewhere, is the mode of travel or the route the first thing that you think about? I would guess not; the first thing you think about is the destination and your reason for going there. Therefore, logically, the first thing that you think about is not a 'how' but a 'what'. For this client to be primarily concerned with the 'how' means that they *already know* what they want the outcome to be, they just can't figure out how to achieve it within the rules of the workplace.

Finally, the word 'handle' is a *kinaesthetic* word. It tells us that the barrier to action in a feeling, and a bad one. We know it's bad because it's causing a nominalisation to appear earlier on in the statement. The feeling acts as a barrier to any further thought on the matter. Good feelings tend not to get nominalised because it's in the person's interest to 'relive' that feeling and enjoy it again.

When people constrain their own thinking, a good way forward is often to have them verbalise their dark aspirations. That will not make them any more likely to act upon them, assuming that you are not dealing with someone who is mentally ill or has a track record of violence. I'm really talking about ordinary people like you and I, people who would love to give that smart-arse in the office their come-uppance if it weren't for the small matter of business etiquette. And of course the legal definition of 'actual body harm'.

I've worked with many managers who had "tried everything" to motivate a failing employee. Everything apart from the one thing that they really wanted, of course, which was to fire the under-performer. But they ruled out that possibility and immediately constrained their thinking. It was that self imposed constraint which caused the problem, not the performance, because the constraint ultimately led to an implied rule which says that no matter what this person does, you can't fire them. From that rule comes a feeling of powerlessness and frustration which adds further strain and ultimately more damage to the working relationship.

In summary, what this client has done is to deal with a problem or conflict at work by thinking the unthinkable which has created a mental loop which leads, inevitably to a 'stuck' feeling and an inability to deal with the problem effectively.

The way forward is to free them from this ever decreasing loop so that they can discover more effective ways to resolve conflict than by internalising and reinforcing their own frustration.

"I get so frustrated that I'm afraid that..."

Any parent knows the feeling of frustration when a child screams "no!" and throws a bowl of pasta across the room or flatly refuses to cooperate with an everyday request.

Effective parents are able to deal with this normal testing of boundaries by predicting and side-stepping the child's behaviour. With tactics such as distraction and patience, some parents seem to cope effortlessly, whilst others get more and more distraught. In some cases, parents are afraid that they might hurt their child, their frustration becoming unbearable.

This client is describing their reaction to the loss of control. When a child is born, it does things pretty much when its parents say so. It goes to bed where they say and when they say (although it might not go to sleep on cue). It eats what they say and it wears what they say. And one day, that child gets old enough to repeat the word that it has heard from its parents from the day that it was born; "no". It is at this point that the parent realises that the child is not a puppet but a free thinking, independent person. Some 'permissive' parents celebrate the child's independence and allow it free reign, which is actually very, very dangerous. A child does not know what is good for it, and thinks only of short term gains. If a parent asks a child if it would like ice cream for breakfast every day, most children up to a certain age will of course say yes. Children, left to their own devices, want to eat sweets, play and have their parents' undivided attention, all day, every day. But that's not feasible. When Daddy goes to work or when Mummy talks to a friend on the phone, the child reacts quite naturally to the withdrawal of attention and demands it back using any means possible; pulling on the parent's hand, screaming, singing, drawing on the wall or 'spilling' paint onto Daddy's suit jacket.

In our client's opening statement, there are three words that we need to examine; 'get', 'so' and 'afraid'. Not 'frustrated'? No, that's the feeling that *results* from the interaction of these other three elements. Frustration is the outcome, it doesn't play a part in the process.

The sentence "I get so frustrated that I'm afraid that..." is grammatically equivalent to "I get frustrated so that I'm afraid that..." and this second version makes the importance of 'so' stand out. 'So' is a sequence word. It tells us about the order in which things happen, and most importantly, it tells us that something has reached a threshold.

"It was so heavy that I needed help to lift it"

"I finished my report so I went home"

"I was so late that I decided to cancel the meeting"

The word 'get' tells us that this process is moving, building. The client isn't just frustrated from the outset, they have to *get* frustrated. That tells us that there is resistance to a course of action, otherwise that thought would rampage through to its conclusion; a behaviour. When I'm thirsty and I imagine a nice cool drink, nothing but my own lethargy stops me from getting a drink. But when that course of action is something that I might reasonably want to avoid, such as completing my tax return, it can take a much longer time for the thought to become action.

When does that thought crystallise into action? When it reaches the threshold indicated by 'so'.

The final piece of the puzzle is 'afraid'. Another kinaesthetic word, it tells us that the barrier to action is a feeling; fear. But fear of what? In the first example, the 'of what' or 'of whom' was hidden by a nominalisation. Here it's hidden by a simple deletion; the client simply stops speaking rather than complete the sentence and speak the unspeakable. The original statement is grammatically incorrect, and the missing grammar tells us that there is a missing half of the statement; thought, but not spoken.

But how would the parent know that the subject of their fear is a viable course of action for controlling a child's behaviour? And how would they know that it's frightening? Because they have experienced it themselves.

Therefore, we have the final piece of the puzzle. Remember that I said that frustration is a result, an outcome. It isn't actually the client's primary emotion; that being *anger*.

Let's put it all together. Parent experiences loss of control, seeks to regain control through violence, feels the fear that he felt as a child and puts a stop to the thought process. The cycle continues, and reinforces itself every time. The client has probably learned some coping strategies for dissipating the feeling of frustration, which may include walking away to take a deep breath, passing the child to its mother to deal with, going off to play golf or even drinking to numb the anger and pain.

It's a sad predicament. The client simply needs a little help coming up with some more effective ways of gaining cooperation from his child. But while he's stuck in this anger/fear cycle, that is very unlikely to happen. In his mind, he has tried everything. In fact, he has tried 'everything' to deal with his frustration, believing that his child's resistance to control is immutable.

The parent would never, ever verbalise his darkest fears because what parent would ever admit to harbouring thoughts of harming their child? This desire to obscure the unthinkable is revealed in the silent second half of the statement.

"I get so frustrated that I'm afraid that... I might hit my child so much that I hurt him, or worse, but it's the only way that I can get him to listen to me."

If you are a parent, you will absolutely understand this heartbreaking contradiction; that the person you love most in the world is, at the same time, the most difficult person to learn to deal with.

Introducing effective parenting strategies is a job for a specialist[4]. What I have illustrated here is how the parent's thought patterns create a prison which can only ever spiral inwards until, one day, the client can contain their frustration no longer. By revealing the cycle, they

---

4   A good book on this subject is Little Angels by Stepheni Smith, CGW Publishing, ISBN 978-0-9565358-6-3

can question some of the fundamental preconceptions that it is based upon, such as:

- I am in control of other people
- My child is challenging my authority
- My child won't listen to me
- My child will starve if he doesn't eat this meal
- My child will never stop crying
- I will turn out like my father before me

When we question our preconceptions, we open our minds for growth.

"I would like to be better at time management"

Again, there are three important elements in this statement, 'would like', 'better' and 'management'.

'would like' presupposes a following 'but...'. The statement sounds like a grammatically complete sentence, but it isn't; it's a sentence fragment.

'better' is a *comparative deletion*, where the object of the comparison is missing

'management' is another nominalisation, and in any case, you can't manage time, you can only manage what you *do* in the time you have available.

The client is comparing their productivity to something, someone or sometime else. They feel that they *should* be more productive, but they're not. The 'but' is the barrier in this statement, creating the loop which is expressed as the nominalisation. A Master Practitioner might respond to this statement in a number of ways:

- "Who or what is more productive than you, or when were you more productive?"
- "What do you want to do with your time?"
- "But.... what? You can't be bothered? You don't want to set yourself up to be given more work?"

The comparative deletion possibly implies an exclusion, such as, "I would like to as productive as Fred, but I'm not Fred so I can't be", although we can't guess at this until we've recovered the object of the comparison.

The Meta Model

The Meta Model deals with Deletions, Distortions and Generalisations, as follows:

Deletions

Something has been removed and must be recovered.

Distortions

Something has been changed and must be changed back to its original form.

Generalisations

Something has been simplified and must be specified. Some generalisations also generalise time, so that a single event becomes projected into the future.

Unspecified Nouns

An unspecified noun deletes either the subject or the object of a verb, forcing the listener to insert their own expectation. The noun might be missing altogether, or it might be replaced with a word like "it" or "thing".

Unspecified Verbs

Either the verb is deleted or its adverb is unspecified, putting the speaker's focus on the end result rather than the way in which it was achieved.

Nominalisation

A nominalisation is a verb that has been turned into a noun, indicating a "stopped" mental process. The object of the verb is also hidden.

Lost Referential Index

This deletion misses out the person or thing that the statement is attributed to, so we cannot test the validity of the statement.

Distorted Referential Index

A common distortion is to say "you" when I mean "I", which implies a dissociation where the speaker sees themselves as if they are looking at a film or in a mirror. The speaker's sense of self becomes detached from the visual representation of themselves.

Simple Deletion

A simple deletion is also known as a "sentence fragment", which may or may not be grammatically correct.

Comparative Deletions

A hidden comparison is implied by words such as 'better' or 'faster'. The deletion hides both the reference point and the criteria for making the comparison.

Complex Equivalence

The speaker takes two unrelated concepts and holds them as equivalent and therefore both true at the same time.

Lost Performative

A performative verb is a statement which is itself an action, such as "I'm telling you to tidy your room". The action in the statement is the telling, not the tidying. A child's response might be, "I'm doing it now", when it would be more accurate to say, "I'm telling you that I'm doing it now". The response is a distortion because the child isn't doing it now, they're only saying so because what they really mean is, "I know you've told me to do it, and I'll do it later", with 'later' meaning 'never'.

Selectional Restriction Violation

The class that something belongs to defines the qualities that it may have; a room may be cold but not sad. A person may be sad but not blue. We often resolve these incongruences by trasnsferring the qualities to ourselves.

Mind Reading

With a mind read, we act as if we know what someone else is thinking or more likely project our own thoughts and attribute them to someone else.

Cause and Effect

The cause and effect implies a relationship in time, so that when one event takes place, a second event will automatically follow.

Presuppositions

Presuppositions are the implied 'facts' which must be held true in order for the sentence to be grammatically correct.

Universal Quantifiers

A type of generalisation, the universal quantifier takes a single example and makes it apply to all cases or at all times, e.g. always, everyone, all, never, nowhere, nothing.

Modal Operator of Necessity

Modal operators modify the verb and are often an indication that the speaker is basing their behaviour on rules, e.g. must, need, should, ought.

Model Operator of Possibility

This modal operator implies choice and options e.g. can, might, may, could.

⁹Beyond Simple Strategies

Imagine for a moment that you are a computer. What is it that defines you as a computer? Is it some physical hardware? A computer with no software would then be the same as one with software, so there must be an element of function or purpose contained within the definition.

What is a computer designed to do?

We might say "Browse the Internet and write letters" or we might say "extend the capabilities of a human being"

One does not preclude the other - they are both true, at different levels of detail.

We could imagine a hierarchy of functions, of purpose:

Extend human capabilities		
Improve memory	Extend communication	Neat writing and drawing
Store photos Remember events Manage tasks	Speak to people Write emails Read news Watch news	Write documents Draw diagrams Paint pictures

Now consider that each of the functions in the bottom row is performed by a software program, and each program has millions of instructions or rules for what to do when the user moves the mouse, presses a key etc.

Each of those basic rules is analogous to a strategy in NLP.

A typical computer has 1,000,000,000 connections or transistors.

A typical human brain has 1,000,000,000,000,000 connections or synapses.

This means that a million computers would be required to provide the same connective power as a single human brain. And those million computers would have all have to be connected to each other.

The challenge for us is to understand what makes a role model by mapping out these simple strategies, and so we need to understand how they all fit together into a hierarchy of perception, behaviour, beliefs and a sense of identity and self awareness.

A strategy must serve a function otherwise it would not have been created. That function, or purpose, or outcome, may be outdated, nevertheless it still defines the strategy. The context or environment within which that strategy was learned is also necessary in order for that strategy to fulfil its function.

Which of the NLP presuppositions describes this?

Changing context

A belief, behaviour or strategy creates a reality around it, and that reality has a whole set of dependencies which have to be maintained in order for the belief to be true.

The effectiveness of a strategy within a context, such as the avoidance of flying within the context of not needing to fly, creates a unique relationship between the strategy, the outcome and the context.

For example:

> I'm afraid of flying. I don't go on holiday anywhere that requires flying, so it isn't a problem. Today, I received an invitation to my best friend's wedding, in Spain. It's really impractical to get there any other way than by flying.
> I want to go but I'm afraid of flying.
> I'm so afraid of flying that I have never been on an aeroplane.
> What can I do?

Do you see what is happening here? The person is behaving as if their model of reality IS reality. Because I think flying is scary I don't fly, in fact I have never flown. It's like a person who says they don't like prawns, having never ate one. I don't like lobster. I never ate it until I tried it on holiday. I was glad I tried it, but I probably won't have it again. This is very different to 'I never eat lobster'.

When we generalise, we don't just generalise within a category e.g. all sales people are the same, we also generalise through time. All sales people are the same because they always have been and always will be.

Because I imagined flying being dangerous in the past, I choose not to fly now, and now has no end point and therefore represents the future.

The person has equated a thought about flying with the experience of flying itself, generalising their inner model outwards onto the world.

Another way to think about generalising through time is that it is always now, therefore past, present and future are all happening at the same time, so we can create causal connections between events that are in reality unrelated, hence our reliance on lucky charms and rituals.

When the context around a belief changes, it can break these connections and the generalisations collapse.

How can you use this in your change work?

Which of the NLP presuppositions does this relate to?

There is a positive intention motivating every behaviour and a context in which it has value

Perhaps if we think in terms of strategies, we could rephrase that presupposition as:

There is an outcome directing every strategy and a context in which it aligns with higher outcomes

In other words, every strategy is useful in that it is directed by and leads to an outcome, when it is in an appropriate context. When that context changes, either the outcome or the strategy need to change.

Alternatively, we can change the context in order to change the strategy. This is the essence of reframing as a change approach.

In fact, if we take these three elements and compare them to NLP as a change methodology, this is what we might end up with:

Can you add some more techniques to the list above?

In order to effect a change in a person's situation, we can change either the strategy, the outcome or the context, and various techniques exist to do this.

For example, if you don't get on with someone at work, your friends might suggest that you either try a different approach with them (change strategy), just focus on getting on with your job (change outcome) or change jobs (change context).

NLP techniques simply bridge the gap between knowing what to do and knowing how to do it.

Well Formed Outcomes

At Practitioner level, you will have learned one of the fundamental techniques; how to set a Well Formed Outcome.

My simple acronym for remembering the Well Formed Outcomes criteria is PURE:

Positive: What you do want?

Under your control: You don't need anybody else; achieving the goal is solely down to you

Real: You can see, hear, feel and perhaps taste or smell the outcome

Ecological: You don't lose anything, or gain anything undesirable, as a result of the outcome

Therefore, we can set an outcome and work through cycles of action and feedback until the result is achieved:

PURE Outcome

Result

Which NLP presupposition describes this cycle?

"All results and behaviours are achievements, whether they are desired outcomes for a given task/context, or not"

9.1 Set an outcome

Set a Well Formed Outcome for something that you can achieve today.

Outcome:

Positive:

Under your control:

Real:

Ecological:

9.2 Work back from an outcome

Ask your partner to list 3 things they have achieved this week. Work back from the result to what the outcome must have been. Choose the 3 results as listed below.

For each of these examples, work back to determine what their outcome may have been, even if it seems contrary to what they say they wanted to achieve.

1. One result which was exactly what they wanted

2. One result which was different from what they wanted

3. One result which was not what they wanted

What can you deduce about outcomes from a person's current situation, and how is this important when you are modelling an intuitive skill?

It's Broken

All too often, you will hear people talk about things that are broken. The TV is broken, the washing machine is broken, the car has broken down and so on. Perhaps we have become so dependent on the labour saving devices that we have created that we just expect everything to work as it is supposed to, and we expect people to do what we expect them to do too.

I want you to get used to asking a new question.

Instead of asking, "What is wrong with it?", ask

"What is it doing?"

Your washing machine is doing something, even if it is not washing your clothes. By asking what is IS doing rather than what it is not doing, you can then compare what it IS doing to what it SHOULD be doing. This is very useful indeed, and is certainly more useful than complaining about the fact that it isn't working.

9.3 What is it supposed to do?

Ask your partner to tell you about something that they own that is currently not working.

Ask them:

What is it doing?

Is that what it is supposed to do?

What is it supposed to do?

From this, deduce what might be preventing the item from doing what it is supposed to do, assuming that they have a clear idea of what it is supposed to be doing!

Let's apply the same approach to coaching.

9.4 What is supposed to happen?

Ask your partner to tell you about something in their life which is not how they would like it to be.

Ask them:

What is happening?

Is that what is supposed to happen?

What is supposed to happen?

From this, deduce what might be preventing what is supposed to be happening, assuming that they have a clear idea of that!

This is the essential difference between remedial and generative change, and it is fundamental to understanding how and why NLP's techniques are used, not to fix problems, but to generate choice.

Incongruence

Earlier, I mentioned sequential and simultaneous incongruence and promised to return to the subject.

Sequential incongruence is where someone gives you contradictory information in a sequence, for example saying that they're not hungry and then picking up a cake.

Simultaneous incongruence is where someone gives you contradictory information at the same time, for example saying yes while shaking their head.

Both of these cases of incongruence reveal conflicting underlying processes which find different channels through which to be expressed. I'm sure that you have dilemmas and difficult choices every day. Some of these you resolve logically, others intuitively. Often, other people are aware of these dilemmas before you are, because they notice your unconscious communication.

You: I must get this report finished

Colleague: Then why aren't you working on it?

You: Erm... I need to do something else first

Colleague: So do you need to finish it or not?

You: Yes, of course, that's what I said

Colleague: It looks to me like you're putting it off

You: Well, I suppose I am in a way...

Colleague: In a way? You're totally procrastinating!

It's far too simplistic to regard incongruence as lying; it is more useful in some situations to regard it as an attempt by your mind to express multiple conflicting intentions or messages at the same time.

"I need to go to the shops but I don't want to go out in the cold"

"I need to go to the doctor but I'm afraid of what he'll say"

"I need to call my friend but I don't really want to go out with her tonight"

Superficially, these examples of incongruence present two conflicting needs; a need to go to the shops and a need to stay warm, for example.

These needs cannot coexist, and one must eventually outweigh the other if action is to be taken. At NLP Practitioner level, we often talk about this in terms of a hierarchy of values, and there are negotiation techniques such as the Squash which serve to bring together conflicting needs in order to encourage action.

However, on closer inspection, we often find something far more interesting. Look at the three examples above; what do you notice is structurally different about the needs in each pair?

I need to go to the shops	but	I don't want to go out in the cold
I need to go to the doctor	but	I'm afraid of what he'll say
I need to call my friend	but	I don't really want to go out with her tonight

↑	↑
These needs are quite practical and physical and are expressed as 'towards' statements	These needs are 'away from' statements, relating to the avoidance of an imaginary outcome

Let's reword these a little:

I need to go to the shops	but	I imagine being cold and not liking it
I need to go to the doctor	but	I imagine what the doctor will say and I don't like it
I need to call my friend	but	I imagine going out and not liking it

If you said any of these conflicting statements to any man in the street, you'd expect him to say, "Well, you don't know that for certain, so there's only one way to find out. Stop whining and get off your backside!"

Maybe at some level, we know that our conflicts are about avoidance or laziness, so we hide them in statements that sound defensible. One remedy is to reverse the statement at the 'but':

I want to stay in the warm	but	I need to go to the shops
I'm afraid it will be bad news	but	I need to go to the doctor
I prefer to stay in tonight	but	I need to call my friend

Now, most people, when expressing these statements would then follow them up with a natural conclusion:

I really want to stay in the warm but I need to go to the shops **so** I'll get it over with and then I can stay in the warm all night.

I'm afraid it will be bad news but I need to go to the doctor **because** then at least I'll know for sure.

I really prefer to stay in tonight but I need to call my friend **and** maybe she'd like to stay in too.

We'll explore these chaining statements in more detail when we talk about modelling belief systems. For now, notice that re-ordering the sequence of beliefs often leads to a spontaneous reorganisation of the person's perceptions and behaviour.

9.5 But...

Ask someone to come up with a conflicting belief statement that has a 'but' in the middle. For example, you might ask them to tell you about something that they've been meaning to do but haven't. They might say, "I need to decorate the spare room but I'd have to move all the furniture out".

Recover the imaginary construction from the second half of the statement:

"When you think about moving all the furniture out, what comes to mind?"

"Oh, it will take ages and it will be dusty"

Now reverse the two halves of the original statement:

"So moving the furniture will take ages and it will be dusty but you need to decorate the spare room?"

Ask the person to comment on their thoughts and feelings about this final, reversed statement.

Metaprograms

NLP metaprograms have been the subject of work by a number of people including Robert Dilts, Rodger Bailey and Shelle Rose Charvet.

You can think of metaprograms as organising patterns, e.g. if you imaging looking at the pieces of a jigsaw puzzle, you might start by sorting them into sky, trees, edges etc. At the highest level, the shape of a piece is an organising pattern, at the next level down, the colour of the piece is an organising pattern. By organising our perceptions, we can handle more information, sort it and make sense of it more easily. This is the fundamental basis, in NLP, of how we make sense of our environment and generate our behavioural responses to it.

Therefore, metaprograms tell us how a person organises their perceptions and how we can influence their behaviour accordingly. Think of them as patterns of deletions, distortions and generalisations.

From a purely behavioural point of view, if an individual automated behaviour is known as a 'program' then a 'metaprogram' could be a program for selecting programs. For example, on your computer, Microsoft Word could be a program, Windows could be a metaprogram. If we understand the metaprograms, we can work at a higher level than simply addressing the individual behaviours. We can organise seemingly different behaviours into generalised patterns and introduce choice at a higher level, thereby increasing flexibility and the effectiveness of change.

For example, eating snacks, fidgeting, chewing pens, being irritable and becoming addicted to Nicotine patches seem like different behaviours at one level, yet at another level they are all responses to a person's attempts to give up smoking. Getting a person to stop chewing pens will only result in the driver for the behaviour generating a different outcome, such as gaining weight from eating snacks.

You can see the similarity between this and (Neuro) Logical Levels, in that both are hierarchical patterns of organisation. To make a change at the level of Metaprogram is analogous to making a change at the Belief or Identity level in that a reorganisation of perceptions at all lower levels takes place at the same time. If we redefine war as protecting our national security then suddenly it becomes acceptable to imprison civilians without trial. Fortunately, not everyone is taken in when politicians try to use this as a justification for human rights violations. Having said that, the author Walter Pitkin proposes that 80% of the population are stupid, although the 20% of us who aren't greatly underestimate the threat posed by the stupid majority.

You may have heard of the phrase 'secondary gain', meaning a beneficial side effect to an undesired behaviour. For example, relaxing is a secondary gain of smoking, as is lung cancer.

I would like you to consider this: secondary gain does not exist. It is an idea created by therapists or coaches to explain why someone does something that is 'bad' for them. Smoking, in itself, is not a bad thing. It leads to some undesirable consequences in the long term, whilst in the short term it has some highly desirable consequences. These short term consequences are a primary gain - they are the primary driver for the behaviour. When the person tries to give up smoking, that driver does not go away. The person does not cease to need to look cool or to be able to relax just because they are now thinking of how to avoid the long term undesirable consequences of their behaviour.

The behavioural view of metaprograms is most apparent in the 'LAB profile' (Language And Behaviour) which proposes to predict behaviour based on a person's language structures.

In the following Metaprogram descriptions, you will find examples of these linguistic structures which I have included because you will come across them many times in NLP training and literature if you have not already done so.

This does not mean that I agree with them...

In 'The Encyclopaedia of Systemic NLP and NLP New Coding', Robert Dilts and Judth DeLozier describe the following categories of Metaprogram:

1. Approach to problems

2. Time frame

3. Chunk size

4. Locus of control

5. Mode of comparison

6. Approach to problem solving

7. Thinking style

Christina Hall incorporates the following Metaprograms in her NLP training:

- Time orientation

- Structures of time

- Direction of motivation

- Active/Passive

- Reference of control

- Chunk size

- Self/Other/We

- Similarity/Difference

- Sensory system focus

In 'Words that Change Minds', Shelle Rose Charvet expands on these. I have not included all of her Metaprograms here for two reasons; firstly I think that many of them overlap so much that they are not worth time in their own right, and secondly I don't think it is valuable to get bogged down in the strict definitions and language patterns because they are so context dependent that to try and categorise someone's personality and behavioural choices would likely take your focus away from the most important aspect of NLP - paying attention to the person in front of you, which leads us full circle back to modelling.

Metaprograms and Modelling

You may choose to model a person's metaprograms in their language as part of your approach to generalising their behaviour. For example, you may discover that a particular corporate culture favours sales people with a particular set of behavioural traits which can be represented as metaprograms.

One way of thinking about metaprograms is to regard them as patterns which organise perceptions, making someone more likely to perceive the outside world in a certain way and therefore respond accordingly. Another way of thinking about metaprograms is to regard them as strategies for selecting strategies. Faced with a need to respond, someone will select an appropriate strategy based on an overall metaprogram or meta-strategy.

The buyers in the retailer had this metaprogram profile:

Procedures	Procedures and reports determine activity
Towards	Goal oriented, works toward a result
People	Focuses on relationships over tasks
Individual	Prefers to take responsibility and make decisions without relying on a team
Internal	Self guided, makes decisions against own internal references
Active	Will not sit and wait to be told what to do

The store managers' profile was slightly different:

Procedures	Creates procedures where non exist to increase the autonomy of store staff
Towards	Goal and result oriented
People	Achieves tasks through relationships
Team	Regards store management as a team effort, but does not lose self in the team, maintains individual responsibilities
External	Feedback and information driven, sees results in staff and store performance
Active	Takes action early, especially to turn interruptions into tasks which can be systemised and delegated

10.1 Understanding profiles

As you read through those two profiles, imagine yourself in those two roles.

A buyer meets suppliers, chooses new products, solves supply problems, negotiates discounts and arranges the layout of the store to optimise sales.

A store manager maintains the efficient operating of the store, managing staff and targets such as revenue and waste.

Imagine yourself in the daily activities of these people, making decision based on the relevant metaprogram elements. For example, in a conflict situation, how would an Internal reference differ from an External one?

What happens if you try out these two profiles on the opposite roles? How would a store manager perform with the buyer's profile, and vice versa?

And how dependent are these profiles on the organisation's culture?

Sensory preference

Does everyone see images of memories inside their heads? Does everyone feel an emotion in the same way, with the same intensity? Does everyone hear a voice inside their head, reading out loud, giving instructions and feedback?

As you might expect, everyone is different. Not only that, but everyone uses all of their senses to differing degrees.

You might think that it's impossible to know if someone is seeing a picture or hearing a voice inside their head but it's actually the easiest of all of the metaprograms to determine.

Listen carefully to what someone says - there will be words in their sentences which aren't part of the content which are called predicates. These predicates are biased toward the person's sensory preference.

For example, if we're talking about having a conversation with someone:

We saw eye to eye	Visual
We clicked	Kinaesthetic
We spoke the same language	Auditory

In order to make sense of information, visual people will construct imagines in their heads, auditory people will check sounds and voice tone and kinaesthetic people will check their feelings to make sure an idea 'feels right'.

We tend to put the two auditory senses together for convenience. The difference is that Auditory Tonal relates to sounds and Auditory Digital relates specifically to language.

Here are some more examples of words to watch and listen out for:

	See	Vision	Sharp
	Picture	Outlook	Background
	Look	Bright	Shine
	Watch	Clear	Reflect
	Magnify	Near	Far
	Perspective	Focus	Eye catching
	Notice	Dark	Distant
	Listen	Quiet	Whistle
	Hear	Amplify	Whine
	Sound	Tell	Roar
	Noise	Resonate	Silent
	Replay	Whisper	Rattle
	Loud	Hum	Tone
	Click	Harsh	Clear

Feel	Push	Down
Touch	Embrace	Ache
Grab	Warm	Gut reaction
Hold	Cold	Queasy
Heavy	Light	Float
Sinking	Contact	Shaky
Fuzzy	Wobbly	Ease

In NLP, the senses are often called **representational systems** because that's what they do - they represent the outside world.

Your conscious awareness includes components both from the outside world and from within your memory, and when we remember something, we use our preferred sensory system to bring the information into that awareness. What do you remember about your first car, or a childhood pet? The sensory system chosen is apparent externally in things like language and also in body posture and eye movements.

Some researchers believe that much of the environment we experience is actually made up of memories so that we can reduce the amount of information we need to process. They propose that most of what we think we see is constructed of memories and expectations, which is exactly the way that digital TV works, only sending changes rather than entire frames of video.

Motivation Direction

Are you motivated by goals or by avoiding problems? Do you avoid unpleasant situations or do you know what you want and go for it? Are you good at identifying all of the potential drawbacks of a plan or do you dive in and find out about the problems later?

The direction of motivation is simply this: do you move towards desirable things or away from undesirable things?

To find our whether a person is motivated by moving towards things they want or by getting away from things they don't want, first ask:

"What do you want in (some area of their life or a decision)?"

Then ask the following question 3 times to get a majority answer (ask each question of the previous answer)

"And what is important for you in (previous response)?"

The answer may include something similar to:

Towards	Away from
To get	To avoid
To have	So I don't have to
To become	To get away from
I want	I don't want

This is useful when motivating a person to perform a task or for changing behaviour. It's pointless telling a 'towards' person that by doing something, he can avoid problems later. It's just as pointless telling an 'away from' person that by doing something she will achieve great things.

It is important to bear in mind that an 'away from' motivation is not bad or negative. Tidying the house because you don't want to see the mess feels just as good as tidying the house so that you can see it nice and tidy. The important thing to determine and remember is the direction of the motivation. Even an away from motivation will have an outcome, and if that outcome was achieved then it was well formed which means that it is positive, which means that an away from motivation still moves towards a goal.

Consider driving from London to Birmingham. At any point, do you notice how many miles it is to Birmingham or how many miles you have travelled from London?

An alternative view (i.e. my opinion) is that an 'away from' motivation, characterised by avoidance behaviour, is in fact a 'towards' motivation where there is some fear or undesirable outcome attached to the goal. In the NLP model of behaviour, we are goal directed, therefore a goal or outcome is always in our focus of attention. We may want to achieve that outcome, in which case our behaviour is congruently aligned with it, or there may be aspects of the outcome that we don't want, in which case our incongruence or avoidance manifests itself as the behaviour described in traditional NLP literature for an 'away from' motivational direction.

Reference Source

Have you noticed how some people just know what it is they want whereas other people are always asking if what they're doing is OK? Some people just don't seem to take any notice of the world around them whilst others are always checking that everyone else is OK. Do you instinctively know when something is right, or do you like to keep 'to do' lists so that you can be sure that everything's finished off?

The source of motivation is: do you use your own internal judgements and benchmarks or do you use other people's?

To find out whether a person is motivated and judged by their own internal ideals and concepts or whether they need external feedback and benchmarking you can ask this question:

"How do you know that what you're doing is right?"

Internal	External
I just know	My boss tells me
	My colleagues tell me
	I tick everything off my to do list
	I have a pile of certificates

This is useful when giving reasons as to why someone should perform a task or change behaviour. If you tell an internal person that they should agree to something because everyone else in the team does, they will say "so what?". If you tell an external person that if they think something's right then that's good enough, they may get quite frustrated.

A very Internal person might not even understand the question, the thought of asking someone else's opinion being so alien to them. Internal people tend to hear instructions as comments - External people tend to hear comments as instructions.

Remember again that this is context specific. When a wife wonders how the bedroom would look with new wallpaper and comes home from work to find her husband redecorating, they may have demonstrated an internal/external relationship which can be reversed in other situations.

A coaching client was recently telling me about how he knows when he does a good job - a question that his manager had asked him. I asked him what they answer was and he said "It's just a feeling of satisfaction", a clearly Internal answer. He then went on to say that the feeling comes from feedback from other people, from seeing the results of what he has achieved. - a clearly External source.

The source of new information always has to come from outside, and a feeling is always generated inside. The decision to act on that information, though, can be biased either internally or externally.

A coaching client recently told us that he knows he is doing a good job when he gets a satisfied feeling..... which he gets when he sees his financial data balancing.

It sounds like his reference criteria is internal, but what you're actually hearing is the end point of his strategy. The start point, as he goes on to say, is external.

Choice

Some people never seem to do things the same way twice. Others seem unable to innovate or create and will continue to do something the same way until external events force them to change. Options thinkers are good at being creative and thinking up new ideas and ways to do things. Procedures thinkers are good at finishing things and following routines. You wouldn't want procedures people in creative jobs and you wouldn't want options people in jobs that were heavily regulated. To find out if a person likes to have many options available at each decision point or if that person needs to follow a set procedure, ask:

"Why did you choose this job/car/house/etc."

Options	Procedures
Modal operators of possibility	Modal operators of necessity
Answers **why**, very quickly with well defined reasons like mental bullet points	Answers **how** the choice came to be
	Tells a story

Useful in understanding how a person will react to rules and work structures. Useful in predicting how a person will react to obstacles. Determines how a person will set objectives and what path will be taken to reach those objectives. An options person would need to always have choices and would be frustrated by set procedures and agenda. A procedures person would find choice and indecision frustrating and would seek out procedures and rules.

Generating possibilities can also be a way of avoiding taking action, relating to an 'away from' motivation direction. A procedural bias can indicate a high degree of motivation or commitment to achieving a goal - the same single minded commitment that can lead to either success in the face of obstacles or complete failure when the person fails to take a changing environment into account.

If you watch TV programs such as Dragons' Den, you will see entrepreneurs presenting their business ideas. Sometimes, an entrepreneur has persevered with their idea despite many setbacks and obstacles, and sometimes, those ideas are innovative and worthy of investment. Other times, the idea is just plain daft and the entrepreneur is told to give it up and do something more useful. When people have invested years of their lives into their ideas, it seems unfair, yet this can be a consequence of their unrelenting drive; procedures, internal, towards oriented.

Sorting & Comparison

This simply relates to whether people first notice the differences or similarities between two different concepts or situations. If you're good at 'spot the difference' puzzles, you have a difference bias. If you're good at making connections, metaphors and analogies, that indicates a similarity bias.

Remember that you have the ability to notice both, it's simply where your attention naturally focuses first, and it's important to us because it enables us to make connections to past and future events that ease the change process.

"What is the relationship between this job and your last job/car/house/etc?"

Difference (Mismatch)	Similarity (Match)	Similarity with exceptions
Different to	Same as	Same as... except for
Compared to	Compared with	
One was...	They were both...	They were both... except...

This is useful in learning and decision making, e.g. a differences person would base a choice on the differences between options.

In order to make a comparison, you have to have at least one internal reference. Even comparing two things 'side by side' means that you have to have a comparison criteria, which involves deletions, distortions and generalisations, as well as an internal reference.

Let's say you're buying apples. You hold two up and work out which one is most ripe. You have a criteria, let's say colour, which lets you know that an apple is ripe. This means that you already know the 'right' colour, and you compare the apples in your hand to that. If you compare the two apples to see which is closest to your desired colour, you have to remember one while you look at the other.

Therefore, you might consider this metaprogram to be about the comparison criteria rather than the method of comparison itself. Noticing similarities is primarily a process of generalisation because in order to group items or experiences, they must be generalised into categories. In order to generalise, you first have to delete what is not relevant and then distort the remainder so that it fits into a higher category.

Sorting for similarities is about matching, and sorting for differences is about mismatching. Either process requires an internal reference point and a set of criteria.

Scope Level

Do you like to see the big picture, or is the devil in the detail? Can you easily work out complex relationships or do you like things to be presented bit by bit?

Do you talk about overviews, missing out all of the detail, or do you assemble the picture starting from the detail and working up?

'General' people will start at the top and work down. They'll give you short, generalised answers and when giving directions will start at the destination and fill in major landmarks. 'General' people are better at identifying the relationships between points of information.

'Specific' people start at the first point of detail and work forwards, so in a complex situation they can get lost. 'Specific' people are good for making sure the details of a plan don't get lost in the overview.

As you can see, the scope metaprogram is about generalisation, and the extent to which someone generalises their experiences. You know what a key looks like, even if you haven't seen every key in the world. You know what a door looks like, and you know how to use one, even if you haven't seen a specific door before. When you first used a hotel room key that looked like a credit card, you had to redefine your category of what keys looked like.

If a person thinks at a low level of detail than this tells you that they have more categories into which to sort their experiences, which means that they are deleting more and distorting and generalising less.

If a person thinks at a high level of detail then this tells you that they are working with fewer categories, which means that they are mostly distorting in order to generalise their experiences.

At a high level of detail i.e. with more generalisations, a person would see these items as 'all keys':

whereas a person operating at a low level of detail would see them as being different.

If you imagine what 'key' means to you, you may picture something that is similar to one of the keys above, or it may be different to all of them, yet you can still recognise those items as keys. Someone operating at a low level of detail would not classify the above objects as keys because they were different to their internal model.

You will hear this process taking place when someone says, "Well, it's *like* a key, but it's not really a key, it's more like a credit card, but you put it in a slot in the door and the door unlocks, so I suppose it's a key really".

The difference seems subtle, but it is an important indicator that the person is creating separate categories for the different keys rather than distorting them and placing them in the same category.

When you hear phrases such as, "They're the same thing", you're hearing the process of distortion in order to generalise. Here's a typical office conversation:

"Anyone want anything from the shop?"

"Could you get me an egg sandwich please?"

Later...

"This is ham and egg salad!"

"Yeah, same thing, isn't it? It's got egg in. Just take the ham out if you don't like it."

"But I'm a vegetarian..."

When we step outside of NLP's metaprograms, we might say that there's a bit of laziness, arrogance and disrespect there too, but that's outside of the scope of this book. If you're interested in these sorts of dynamics, you might like to read Revelation by Peter Freeth and Stepheni Smith, which investigates the business impact of lies, hidden agendas and manipulation.

10.1 Metaprogram Profiling

Interview three people and pick out their metaprogram preferences for a particular context, remembering that if you change context, the profile may change.

Remember that these are preferences, not traits, so these aren't an either/or categorisation but a spectrum of possibilities.

Name:	Context:		
Sensory preference	V	A	K
Motivation	Towards		Away from
Reference	Internal		External
Choice	Options		Procedures
Sorting	Same	Except	Difference
Scope	General		Specific

Name:	Context:		
Sensory preference	V	A	K
Motivation	Towards		Away from
Reference	Internal		External
Choice	Options		Procedures
Sorting	Same	Except	Difference
Scope	General		Specific

Name:		Context:	
Sensory preference	V	A	K
Motivation	Towards		Away from
Reference	Internal		External
Choice	Options		Procedures
Sorting	Same	Except	Difference
Scope	General		Specific

Name:		Context:	
Sensory preference	V	A	K
Motivation	Towards		Away from
Reference	Internal		External
Choice	Options		Procedures
Sorting	Same	Except	Difference
Scope	General		Specific

Metaprograms - an Alternative View

Having explored Metaprograms as they have been described in NLP literature, I would now like to present you with a new controversial, opinion on the subject.

There is only one metaprogram. All of the others can be explained within the context of a single principle of operation.

Your attention can be outwardly focused, on real time outside events, or it can be inwardly focused, on internal memories and simulations. All of the metaprograms can be described as aspects or consequences of this shift in focus.

Real time events are always outside, always unknown, full of possibilities and uncertainty. We aim to control the unpredictable world through our fears, rituals, dreams, self help training programs, rules, laws, gurus, religions, horoscopes, lucky charms, incantations and corporate visualisation workshops.

Unfortunately, despite the best efforts of the people selling you these predictions, the outside world still doesn't quite behave as you would like it to. Specifically, the people in the outside world don't behave how you would like them to.

Therefore, options and choices always lie in the outside, external , real time world. Whether to go this way or that way, climb this tree or cross that river, eat this fruit or that vegetable, the ability to analyse choices conferred significant evolutionary advantages. We could assess a number of options and incorporate multiple criteria into decisions. I know there's food by the watering hole, but there was a lion there yesterday so I think I'll head to the woods instead.

The internal world is one of certainty. I can distinctly remember the feeling of running away from the lion, and I know exactly how to do that again, should the need arise. Procedures are certain, sequences, memories, internal and in the past.

Towards and away from are about comparisons, and in order to make a comparison, only one of the criteria can be external. Compare this character $\mathcal{G}$ with this character $\mathcal{G}$. You can't focus on both at the same time, so you hold one in memory whilst you look at the other. Therefore, comparisons are always internal and therefore in the past. Towards and away from are behavioural responses to the result of that comparison.

Equally, sorting by similarity or difference is a result of a comparison. Whether you notice the similarity or the difference first depends on the category that you put the first item in, and the comparison is made to either an internal or external reference. This apple is the same as one I ate yesterday, or it is different. If its appearance is close enough to group with the memory of yesterday's apple then I have noticed the similarity. If it is different enough then it might be rotten, or it might not be an apple at all - another evolutionary advantage. We learn which characteristics are worth comparing, and if you go to the supermarket and watch people buying fruit and vegetables, you will see these comparisons and criteria in action.

As babies, we become accustomed to either having our needs met by a carer, in which case we feel safe relying on someone else, or we become accustomed to not having our needs met, in which case we feel safe when we rely on ourselves. Perhaps this bias results in a focus of attention on either internal or external needs and resources?

Parents have a tough job; they mostly want to meet their child's needs, but they also have to ensure the child becomes self sufficient. This is a difficult balance to get right, and perhaps there is no 'right', only some kind of developmental outcome that allows the child to become a socially functional adult.

Look through the Metaprograms and ask yourself how each one can be described as an aspect of an internal or external focus of attention. Finally, consider how this fits into a perceptual process of deleting, distorting and generalising.

¹¹Modelling Systems

Success Factor Modelling

Robert Dilts is probably the most well known NLP modeller, having modelled people such as Walt Disney and Albert Einstein and produced models of generic skills such as leadership and creativity.

Dilts' Success Factor Modelling approach requires that you find a number of people who appear to share a common skill or talent. The whole modelling process is as follows:

- Interview the individual

- Interview the people they work with or relate to

- Watch them in their normal environment to confirm the model

- Check the model against their peers to benchmark their performance

- Check the model against your own peers to check current research or thinking

- Check the model against the individual or organisation's vision - their stated future direction

- Check the model against the individual or organisation's past - their legacy or habits

From all of these separate models you can then refine a model of the specific skill that can be used by anyone to achieve the same results.

The book 'Alpha Leadership' by Dilts, Deering and Russell contains a good example of Dilts' Success Factor Modelling as applied to modern leadership skills.

Modelling Belief Systems

'Expert Systems' are software programs which emulate human decision processes, and you will find them in call centres, diagnostic systems and so on. Software engineers interview humans and develop decision trees which guide a user through a decision making process.

For example, your computer might have a troubleshooter program that pops up and gives you advice when something goes wrong. It makes a suggestion, then asks if it fixed the problem. If not, it makes another suggestion. This is a very simple example of a decision making program that contains some basic diagnostic knowledge.

Jonathan Altfeld combined this approach with NLP strategy modelling to create what he calls 'Knowledge Engineering', which he used to run training programs in. You can still buy a home study Knowledge Engineering kit from his website at www.altfeld.com

Essentially, we need to regard beliefs as specialised rules about responses and behaviour, and if we regard rules as elements of strategies then we can regard the modelling of a set of beliefs as a more complex application of NLP strategy modelling.

For example, knowing whether to shake someone's hand is a strategy, you also have a set of rules for it and we could call those rules a set of beliefs about greeting people. For our purposes, these terms are interchangeable.

11.1 Complex strategies

Consider again the example of shaking hands. List as many different criteria as you can that would influence your decision to shake someone's hand:

On one hand, this may seem unnecessarily detailed. On the other hand, if we want to truly understand and replicate a skill, we have to understand exactly how it works, otherwise we risk missing something important. We risk shaking hands in a situation that isn't quite right and becoming embarrassed. That's a minor risk, perhaps, and one that we can learn from, so the model is always the starting point that we have to integrate into our own experience and build on with future experiences.

It's all very well teaching someone how to shake hands, but that skill is useless without teaching them when to shake hands.

Robert Dilts proposed a 3 part structure to beliefs:

IF > THEN > MEANS

IF someone is holding out their hand to me THEN I shake their hand which MEANS that I know how to behave in social greeting situations.

Or it could mean a number of other things, in different contexts. If someone states a belief, such as 'I am socially adept' then we could ask them how they know that, how that belief manifests in their behaviour. This enables us to work backwards from the belief to the underlying programs or strategies.

We also have beliefs that influence the operation of other beliefs, for example, I get up early, except if it's a weekend.

Remember that the usefulness of any model is contained within the purpose of the model. If we are modelling in order to replicate results then the test of the model is that it allows other people to replicate the subject's results.

We're not aiming to clone a person - only to find a way to transfer and integrate a specific skill of theirs to other people. Therefore, the level of detail that you go into is determined by the results of this process.

For example, let's say you're modelling a high performing sales person. You observe him at his desk and you notice that the first thing he does is get a pen and scribble on a pad of paper which he then leaves to one side. The behaviour seems irrelevant, so you ignore it.

If you ask him why he did that, what might he say?

How about, "I want to make sure I have a working pen and some paper to hand so if a customer calls, I am always ready to make notes".

Now, that sounds interesting. Why does he do that? What does this rule mean?

"It's all part of giving a professional image"

Another rule. What does it mean?

"Well, the first impression is the most important thing"

So by investigating a seemingly irrelevant behaviour, we learn something very valuable. If you were to then ask for other ways in which he ensures he makes the best first impression possible, you will learn more rules and strategies that you can teach to other sales people.

Once again, we can start modelling at the highest level and from that work down through a hierarchy of beliefs, rules and behaviours in order to understand how the role model's experiences, goals and behaviours fit together. From this, we can see how different behaviours in different contexts are linked, and are examples of the same overall approach.

We can now regard Behaviour, Capability and Beliefs as levels within the overall hierarchy of rules, beliefs, behaviours and strategies.

How we distinguish between one and another is simply a matter of current focus, i.e. Behaviour is what the person is doing now, and that current focus is an example of a current Capability and Belief which we can use to elicit other behaviours.

With our scribbling sales person, we can ask for other examples of how they ensure they make a good first impression, using an observed behaviour to deduce a set of higher level beliefs which in turn enable us to discover other behaviours which we may not have observed directly.

I have said many times that "Why?" is not a useful question in coaching because it elicits reasons rather than causes. In other words, when you ask why someone did something, what you get is an answer to the question, but it will probably not tell you anything about the actual causes and criteria at the time of whatever it is they did.

In modelling, the question "Why?" will, as usual, elicit an answer beginning with "Because..."

Where this is not generally useful in coaching or change work, because the reason embeds and reinforces the behaviour that we want to change, it is useful in modelling because it enables us to work backwards to the rules that determine the behaviour.

"Because" tells you that you are hearing the end of a sequence, a strategy, and what you hear after the word 'because' is the rule or belief. This doesn't give us the cause, but it does give us their reasoning, which is exactly what we want because it is their unique mindset that we are modelling.

So that →

Phrases such as 'so that', 'and then', 'which leads to' etc. tell you that you have just heard the rule or belief and what you are about to hear is the consequence or result of it. "So" oftens gets moved around in grammar, but its meaning stays the same. "It was raining so hard that..." is equivalent to "It was raining hard so that..." in that speaker is telling us two crucial pieces of information; firstly that something happened next, and secondly that there was a triggering event or threshold. "It was raining so hard that I stayed at the office for a while longer". This tells us that the speaker made a decision, and a decision is based on a rule, and that rule is based on a threshold about what to do when it's raining. If you listen carefully, you'll hear thresholds all around you:

"I miss you so much (that I could cry)"

"The system is so overloaded that it's going to fail"

"The book was so good that I couldn't put it down"

But/Except ↗

But and except tell us negative exceptions to the strategy. "I always... except if", "I usually... but when".

When a rule reaches an exception, the person doesn't stop in their tracks, they branch to another rule, for example:

"I start work on the report but then the phone rings so I answer it..."

So you can hear a 'but' as an interruption to a strategy and another strategy beginning.

Which means ↑

Rules exist in a hierarchy, and a chain of decisions will often branch into a series of lower level decisions, just like a computer program branches into a 'subroutine' which can easily be repeated for common tasks.

When a speaker signals a shift to a higher level of belief or rule, you'll hear phrases such as "which means" and "so, obviously".

"Which means" tells you that a number of rules have been grouped together into a common process, for example:

"The door was open, and his coat wasn't on his chair, and his computer was on, which meant that it was OK for me to go and check his emails."

"It was raining, and I had a lot of paperwork to carry, and I really had to be there on time, so obviously I had to take a taxi."

This could either be a rule for taking a taxi versus public transport, or it could be a rule for justifying an expense claim. Either way, the speaker stacks a number of more specific rules inside another more general one.

Coaching with Beliefs

Being able to navigate through a belief system is very useful when coaching. When you want to explore the mental processes that underpin a person's behaviour, you can control the conversation using the very words that they would use to signal branches in a decision process.

When I say that you can control the conversation, I don't mean that you are leading the person to a particular conclusion, because that would not be coaching. Think of yourself as an investigator, searching through surveillance videos to find a series of key events. You need to be able to pause, move forwards and backwards and take snapshots that you can assemble into a simplified sequence. The content is the same, the events are the same. Your ability to control the conversation simply gets to that result more effectively than just letting the client talk freely and hoping that you can pick up some clues here and there.

Here's an example of how you can use this method of to determine an underlying belief structure. The reason for doing this is simple; when a pattern of behaviour repeats itself over the course of a person's lifetime, what they experience is the same underlying process playing out in different situations; relationships, career changes and so on. The scenery and the actors are different each time, but the story remains the same. In Transactional Analysis, these underlying structures are called 'scripts', which are analysed at length in order to understand their role in a person's life and present opportunities to make better informed choices. The NLP view is slightly different, in that the underlying structure of behaviour can be changed without analysis of the events that created that structure. I'm not saying that either of these approaches is right, I'm merely comparing them for your viewing pleasure.

In this example, the client repeats a pattern of behaviour where they enter a new relationship or job with great enthusiasm, only to later discover that they are not valued or respected, which leads them to move on to 'greener pastures'.

"I'm so unhappy about being undervalued at work."

"So unhappy that?"

"That I'm thinking of leaving."

"But?"

"But I'm worried that this is a phase I often go through."

"So?"

"So I'm starting to wonder if it's something about me, the way I'm seeing things."

"Because?"

"Because when I look at my CV, I feel that I've moved jobs too often in the last few years."

"Because?"

"I start to feel like I'm being taken for granted, that they don't value me any more."

"Because?"

"I find that people start to change their attitude towards me, stop making an effort, try to take advantage of me or they're just inconsiderate."

"Which means?"

"Well, I used to say that people make an effort at first, but then they get bored of me. But I'm starting to wonder if it might be at least partly down to something I'm doing."

In this conversation, do you see the way that the client's thinking moves forwards, backwards, up and down? "Because?" moves the client's thinking back to a preceding rule, so that we can start to understand the conditions that must be in place for the situation to progress to the point where the client wants to move on to a new employer or relationship. If you have studied Transactional Analysis, you'll recognise some scripts in there too. Another way to compare the two approaches is that TA is concerned more with content than process, while NLP is concerned more with process than content. However, in reality a client must give you content in

order for you to be able to deduce process, so
value.

I'm going to run through that conversation
time with some comments that might expl___ _____
going on, and might certainly echo what you yourself
thought as you read it the first time.

"I'm so unhappy about being undervalued at work."	"So" indicates a threshold. Instead of asking why they feel that way or what is happening, we want to find out about the threshold.
"So unhappy that?"	
"That I'm thinking of leaving."	"Thinking" means that something is stopping them, otherwise they would be leaving, not thinking about it. "Thinking" is the primary verb here, so don't be distracted by "leaving".
"But?"	
"But I'm worried that this is a phase I often go through."	"But" gives us the exception to what they would have done on previous occasions. "So?" moves them forwards along that branch of thinking.
"So?"	
"So I'm starting to wonder if it's something about me, the way I'm seeing things."	In the past, they wouldn't have been having this conversation because being undervalued would have been "reality" and therefore not up for discussion. "Because" moves back to a preceding step.
"Because?"	

"Because when I look at my CV, I feel that I've moved jobs too often in the last few years."

A feeling is the trigger for the self doubt that has led to this conversation. "Because" moves to a preceding step.

"Because?"

"I start to feel like I'm being taken for granted, that they don't value me any more."

"Start to" means that something came before that feeling and triggered it, "because" moves back to find out more about that trigger.

"Because?"

"I find that people start to change their attitude towards me, stop making an effort, try to take advantage of me or they're just inconsiderate."

The client is now mind reading, so we have arrived at a point in the process which must be under their control because they have chosen what to deduce from other people's actions.

"Which means?"

"Well, I used to say that people make an effort at first, but then they get bored of me. But I'm starting to wonder if it might be at least partly down to something I'm doing."

"Which means?" moves up and the client then begins to acknowledge a level of insight into their mind reading. Control is fundamental to change, so if the person is to change their world, they must focus on what they are in control of.

As you can see, the primary input from the coach is to steer the client's thought process in order to explain the belief system which underpins their perception and behaviour. Some people say that beliefs are a filter through which we experience the world; whether today is a good or a bad day depends entirely on how you face the day, not on what 'really' happens to you. For beliefs to function in this way, they cannot be arbitrary, intangible aspects of your psyche, they must be highly organised systems that have a deterministic structure. Whilst they may be complex, they are by no means unpredictable.

¹²Logical Levels

You've already seen that beliefs exist in a matrix with each belief or rule acting as a decision point which branches on to other rules. A concept that has been incorporated into much NLP training is that of 'Neurological Levels', usually abbreviated to 'Logical Levels'. While there is some contention about its history and validity, you can use the logical levels hierarchy to identify specific behaviours to model, starting at the level of role model, such as 'high performing sales person' or 'leader' and working down into specific behaviours that form part of that identity. By approaching it in this way, you ensure that the behaviours you model are aligned with each other and relevant. For example, you might model a leader's ability to communicate vision as well as their ability to response to setbacks, both of which may be examples of their beliefs about their relationship with other people.

Certainly, the concept of 'personal effectiveness' is very strongly linked with a sense of alignment between a person, a place and a task or activity. When I am doing something that I believe in, I am skilled in and I believe is appropriate for me and my current situation, it is fairly obvious that I will perform more effectively than when I'm doing something that I don't feel that I'm very good at, or isn't really my job. People in all walks of life and in all jobs find a way to excel, to "make it their own", and these are typically the people that you will be choosing as role models. The key isn't that a person is a "born leader", it is that they have found a way to align their self concept with their environment and goals. People are not born to be leaders or doctors; they have a set of life experiences which predispose them to succeeding in certain jobs because that is the way that those jobs work. But many people fail at those jobs too, because their concept of what the job is 'about' is different to what is required in practice. For example, a child who loves small cuddly animals dreams of being a vet, only to find that their love of cuddly animals makes the job very stressful and upsetting for them, because vets aren't usually paid to cuddle; they're paid to poke animals with needles and other implements. They care about the animal's well being, but not in the same way as they did as a child. The people who make that transition succeed as vets, the people who don't give up and take a different career path, saying, "I just wasn't cut out to be a vet". Even the phrase "cut out" implies that it is nature, not nurture, which determines your ideal career.

Logical Levels is a hierarchy of categories into which we can organise statements made about ourselves. "I am writing" and "I am a writer" are very different statements, even though they sound similar. If you are a parent, consider when you became one. Was it at the moment of your first child's birth, or was it before, or afterwards? The acceptance of an identity rarely comes at the same time as the behaviour which is the hallmark of that identity. When did you become a driver, or a manager, or a reader? Was it different to when you started driving, managing or leading?

| System | The system that you are part of, e.g. a culture, market, community or spiritual belief system |

| Identity | Your identity, how you label yourself, e.g. plumber, manager, father, king, straight, optimistic |

| Beliefs | What you know to be true, e.g. 'I am a good manager', 'I'm honest', 'You have to get what you can' |

| Capability | What you can do, e.g. 'I can drive', 'I know how to manage people' |

| Behaviour | What you are doing, e.g. 'I am reading', 'I am working' |

| Environment | Where you are, e.g. 'in the office', 'on a train', 'at home', 'it's warm' |

Therefore, you could say, "I'm in the car", "I'm driving", "I can drive", "I'm a good driver" or "I am a motorist". All essentially comment on the same experience, but they each tell us something different about your frame of reference, in that each level is a category within which other, lower level categories exist or are implied. You can see that, "I'm a parent" is a much broader statement than, "I'm helping my daughter with her homework", the latter being one behaviour which a parent would engage in.

Whilst Logical Levels is a hierarchy of categories, those categories don't exist 'out there' in the world and they are perhaps better understood as a function of our ability to categorise information. Can you name a type of farm animal? A cow? Now name a type of cow. A farm animal is a valid example, along with toy, pet or friesian. Our mental dexterity means that we can create an arbitrary structure and then turn it on its head just as easily.

Robert Dilts defined a mentor as being a role model at the identity level, so if we set out to model a mentor we are essentially starting at the highest level and all that it encompasses, which is obviously very broad.

If you ask the role model to start at the Behaviour level, i.e. "what do you do?" then they will typically identify only the behaviours that they are consciously aware of, and these will often have very little to do with what differentiates them from average performers in their field.

Earlier, we looked at the relationship between a strategy, the outcome that directs it and the context that it exists within. We could map this onto the logical levels hierarchy as follows:

Logical levels is useful in modelling because a role model will have different levels of awareness of what they do, and we can record those levels of awareness using the Logical Levels framework. You'll see how this works in the example modelling study towards the end of this book.

If you are interested in learning then you will no doubt have come across this theory, developed by Noel Burch of Gordon Training International in the 1970s:

The idea is that when you learn a new skill, you start off not knowing that you're not very good at it. You then realise that you're not very good at it, then you learn to become good at it, but you have to think about it. Finally, you end up not having to think about it. If you can drive a car, ride a bicycle, play a musical instrument or read then you may remember how it felt to go through this process.

Whilst this theory has been disputed, as theories generally are, it is hard to deny that mastering a skill requires a stage of conscious learning where you have to think about what you're doing, followed by a realisation that you can perform the skill automatically without having to remind yourself of what to do.

We can draw some comparisons between this theory and that of Logical Levels. At the Behaviour level, someone is aware of what they are doing or not doing. At the Capability level, they are no longer thinking about the skill itself, instead their focus being on a broader set of abilities. At the Belief and Identity levels, their focus is simply on the end result that the behaviour achieves.

I think it's fair to say that learning is a fairly consistent, universal process which has been researched from many different angles, producing many different theories. Yet these theories are not mutually exclusive and are therefore facets of the same underlying principles.

As I mentioned in the section on Kolb's learning styles, the more you understand about learning from broadest possible perspective, the more easily you will be able to replicate excellence using the modelling tools in this book.

12.1 Logical Levels modelling

In 3s, 15 minutes each, 45 minutes total.

Use the Logical Levels hierarchy to work from a role model's Identity down to specific behaviours.

Start with some specific ability that you want to model.

Identity Who are you when you do this? How do you see yourself when you do this? What are you aiming to achieve when you do this?
Beliefs What makes a good [Identity]? What is important for a good [Identity]? What do you believe about yourself when you do this? How do you know that you're good at this?
Capabilities What skills do you have that enable you to do this? How did you learn how to do this? Do you set specific outcomes when you do this? How do you know you've achieved what you want?
Behaviours What specifically do you do? How could you teach me to do this?
Environment Where and when do you do this?

¹³Neurologic

London taxi drivers were placed in a brain scanner and the blood flow in their brains was monitored while they calculated routes[5]. From this, the experimenters discovered that a part of a taxi driver's brain is more active than those of other people. The learning process that they go through - 'The Knowledge' - increases the number of connections in a part of their brain that we all have, but which for them contains details of the 25,000 streets of London plus countless landmarks, offices, bars, congestion points etc. So the scientists know which part of a taxi driver's brain is used to calculate a route, but this does not constitute knowing how they do it.

Make sure you read the article 'Mirror Neurons and the Simulation Theory of Mind Reading' by Gallese and Goldman[6]. They evaluate evidence for our ability to infer others' internal emotional states as well as the mental processes behind their behaviour. This is proposed as the basis of our unconscious modelling ability, the ability to emulate others, as you will see very young children doing naturally in order to learn to walk, talk etc.

One thing that we do know is that the human brain is an incredibly complex structure. Traditional thinking is that nervous system cells are never replaced once they die or are damaged, yet even this thinking is changing. Certainly, where brain cells themselves may not regenerate readily, the connections between them are highly adaptable.

In the past, neurologists thought that regionalised brain function meant that specific cells were responsible for

---

5   Recalling Routes around London: Activation of the Right Hippocampus in Taxi
      Drivers, Maguire, Frackowiak & Frith, The Journal of Neuroscience, 15 Sept. 1997
6   Trends in Cognitive Sciences, 1998

specific tasks and functions. Over many years, scientists mapped areas of the brain; sensory areas, motor areas, areas for emotions, language, short and long term memory and so on. Yet there are many cases where people recovered from severe head injuries, not because their brain cells regenerated but because areas of their brain changed function as connections were reorganised.

Look up the following names on the Internet to see two remarkable stories:

Phineas Gage

In 1848, a 25 year old construction foreman named Phineas Gage became famous for having a hole in his head. While working on a railroad project in Vermont, he experienced a severe brain injury when a metre long tamping iron was shot through his skull by a stick of dynamite. He lived to tell the tale - with a very different personality.

Dr. Lionel Feuillet

A 44 year old French man's brain had been reduced to little more than a thin sheet of actual brain tissue, due to the buildup of fluid in his skull ["He was a married father of two children, and worked as a civil servant"]. In July 2007, Fox News quoted Dr. Lionel Feuillet of Hôpital de la Timone in Marseille as saying: "The images were most unusual... the brain was virtually absent."

To return to the relevance of this to modelling, we know that there are connections between brain cells, and that these connections can cause other cells to activate or inhibit their activation. We also know that computer circuits operate in a similar way. Computer circuits, based on elements known as transistors have tended to work in a strict on/off way, whereas brain connections seem to be much more flexible, behaving in a way that we might describe as on/off/maybe. Recent developments in the application of quantum physics to computing have created potentially powerful quantum computers that have very similar logic states.

Since the number of these connections between brain cells appear to be limitless, this implies that there are limitless possibilities for rules and therefore beliefs, experiences, learning etc.

In a computer, there are essentially two types of logical connections; AND and OR. These can also be negated to NAND and NOR. We also have the concept of eXclusivity.

AND - if **all** of the inputs are active, activate the output

OR - if **any** of the inputs are active, activate the output

NAND - if **all** of the inputs are active, deactivate the output (Not AND)

NOR - if **any** of the inputs are active, activate the output (Not OR)

XOR - if **any** but **not all** of the inputs are active, activate the output (eXclusive OR)

Using these connections, we can create interconnected rules which support or inhibit other rules and in doing so create a behavioural output from a set of complex criteria.

We can draw circuit diagrams for logic circuits such as those in your computer or mobile phone. Here's a very simple one from a computer that was built over 30 years ago:

But don't worry, we are not going to draw a circuit diagram for your brain. We'll start with something a little simpler.

In circuit diagrams like the one above, there are specific symbols for the different logic gates. We won't bother using those, we just need to think about the basic principle of how we can represent the connections which form the basis of a strategy, decision or behaviour.

Here's an example for telling the time, where the black dot negates the input:

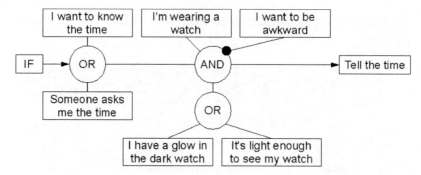

In other words, if either I want to know the time, or if someone asks me the time, and I'm wearing a watch, and I can see it, and I'm not being awkward, then I'll tell the time. Being awkward would mean that when the person asks, "Can you tell me the time?", I answer, "Yes".

Here is a different way of representing a belief system; this one is a decision strategy for having some chocolate:

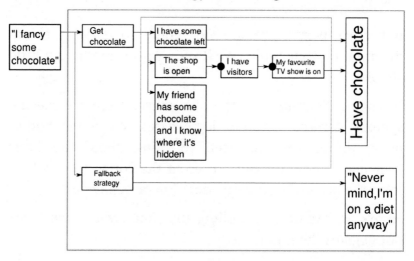

This is a decision strategy, so the entry and exit points are external. Feeling hungry, taking action to get chocolate and saying that you didn't want any anyway are all external to the thought process or strategy.

The final OR is an exception to the whole strategy. In computer programming, there are If... THEN statements such as IF this condition THEN do this action. The ELSE statement provides a way out for if an unforeseen IF condition exists. So in the above example, if I can't easily get some chocolate then the ELSE or 'otherwise' outcome is to justify why I didn't want or need chocolate anyway. This is a common control strategy; if you can't get what you want, maintain control by not wanting it anyway.

Overall, that makes this a strategy about getting chocolate embedded within a strategy for self gratification, which therefore implies that there is some guilt attached to having chocolate in the first place, and therefore some merit in not having it.

Incidentally, having read through this decision strategy in 'slow motion', are you now thinking that you would quite like some chocolate? Well you can't have any, I've eaten it all.

As you can see, every strategy is nested within another. This is why it is so important to be very specific about what you are modelling.

The rule of thumb is that if you reach an external step, you're no longer dealing with a strategy. A strategy is a purely mental decision process; a way of selecting one course of action from a range of possibilities.

13.2 Designing logic 1

Using these simple logical connections, design a logic circuit that produces a cup of tea.

13.3 Designing logic 2

Now design a logic circuit to perform the decision strategy that you modelled from someone earlier.

¹⁴Creativity

One of the most coveted skills in business is that of 'creativity', and a great deal of academic research has been done in this area, which I won't repeat here. Instead, I want to discuss a very specific type of creativity, which I have found is what most people are really talking about in business when they say that they want people to be more creative. My experience over the past 27 years in business is that when managers say they want people to be more creative, what they really mean is that they want people to solve problems more quickly and not be constrained by obstacles or cultural limitations.

Of course, any strength, when applied to excess, can become a weakness. Coming up with exciting new ideas is fine, but sooner or later, someone needs to turn them into operational activities. Determination is a good quality until it becomes stubbornness.

It turns out that the techniques that we can use for modelling talents can also be applied to increasing creativity, particularly in the area of problem solving.

The most common obstacle to creativity is when people get stuck down a particular line of thinking, having assumed that one aspect of a situation is fixed. Creative insights come when someone turns the situation on its head and questions what had previously been held to be an immutable fact. Much research has been done in this area, producing such theories and models as 'groupthink[7]' and SCAMPER[8]. The 'Five Whys[9]' technique aims to get problem solvers to work backwards in a cause and effect chain, asking "Why?" five times. This technique works

7   Irving Janis
8   Bob Eberle
9   Sakichi Toyoda

very well in mechanical systems that have deterministic operating rules, but very badly in human systems where people make up the rules as they go along.

Asking "Why did the machine fail" can generate a variety of responses, from, "Because the planned maintenance was not carried out so the driveshaft seized up" to "Because you're always demanding that we work longer shifts and I've told you a thousand times that something's got to give and those idiots in finance are always stopping us from making the right investments and in any case we can either stand around here talking about it or you can let me get on with my job." The latter reason can loosely be translated as, "I didn't do the planned maintenance properly because I'm lazy".

When applying systemic problem solving tools to human systems, the results can be unreliable because human beings may not be straight with you. Defensiveness, avoidance and misdirection will plague you if you try to apply a simplistic approach. By looking at belief systems, it doesn't really matter whether someone gives you straight answers or not, as both are equally meaningful.

When you want to foster creativity or solve a complex problem, you can use the basic modelling techniques listed here to understand the system within which the creative approach is required. Any behaviour which leads to a consistent result is a skill, whether or not we like that result in a particular context or not, and you can model 'failure' as easily as 'success', and often with more interesting results. By mapping out the intuitive processes of a system, you can easily uncover the hidden assumptions that would otherwise stifle creativity.

¹⁵Installation

And now we reach the important bit. Having created a model, how do we turn it into something useful? Perhaps a new business process or an activity on a training course?

The process of modelling has turned a complex behaviour into a strategy, a series of decisions, by abstracting a behaviour from the context within which it was modelled. You will have achieved this by comparing counter examples, external perspectives and by testing your theories. What you will end up with is a strategy which can then be taught to someone else, or 'installed', as we might say.

Let's say that you modelled someone's skill for being afraid of spiders? Why would anyone want to learn that skill? Remember that the talent is totally independent of the context or result. A talent for being afraid of spiders is actually a talent for distorting sensory data in order to produce a heightened emotional response. Imagine you're in a sales meeting, hoping that your customer will buy something from you. Would a talent for producing a heightened emotional response be useful?

Essentially, when you want to install a strategy, you need to turn it into a series of steps that a person can practice explicitly. You can also expect them to modify it so that it fits into their existing skills and experience. You also need to ensure they are clear on the outcome and purpose, and the success criteria for the strategy.

Rituals and Incantations

I recently enquired about holidays in a High Street travel agent's office, and at the end of the conversation, she asked if she could call me in a few days time to follow up. As I always do with sales calls, I said, "Yes, of course". After all, if you want to find out what the best sales people do, you have to spend time with sales people.

As promised, a couple of days later, the assistant called and asked if I had made a decision about my holiday. I said that I hadn't and she said that if I needed anything, don't hesitate to call, or something equally vague.

Just a few weeks later, exactly the same thing happened in a mobile phone shop. The sales assistant was decidedly disinterested throughout the conversation and only perked up to tell me I was wrong about a mobile phone that I used to own because he'd had three. Bowing to his superior knowledge, I was happy for him to call back in a few days time to see if I had made my mind up. Once again, the box on his sales sheet was ticked and I received my call. His disinterest was much the same as the experience in the shop just a few days earlier.

What's going on? Is this a coincidence?

A few years ago, I visited a car dealership to look at a particular model. The salesman told me, through the gift of non-verbal communication, that I really wasn't worth five minutes of his valuable time. Tabloid newspapers don't read themselves, you know. As I looked over the car, he seemed to be doing his best to make me feel like an unwelcome visitor, and when I handed back the keys, he summoned up all of his enthusiasm and muttered, "So, can you see yourself sitting in a new Peugubishi?"

I said, "No", and left the dealership.

Here's what happens. A company's sales trainers go out and spend time with the staff in the branches. When they see someone performing well, they watch what they do. When they think they've figured out a particular phrase or behaviour, they build it into the sales process and teach it to new sales recruits. By the time the behaviour gets to the corporate classroom, it has lost any glimmer of a talent that it once held and has been reduced to a line in a script, a letter in an acronym, a step in a sales process.

Once upon a time, there was a salesperson who made follow up calls and, as a direct result, they sold more of their product or service.

Another salesperson discovered that certain language patterns, used in hypnosis and 'corporate visioning' led the listener to imagine themselves using the product or service, and that imagined experience would create emotional engagement which would make the listener more likely to become a buyer.

Whatever the 'technique' is, there are fundamentally two reasons why these approaches work:

1. The salesperson genuinely cares about the sale
2. No-one else is doing it

If you take the behaviour and reduce it to a script that is then beaten into a classroom of sales recruits, what you will end up with is something that the sales people only do *because they have been told to*. And that is a recipe for failure.

Of course, when a company has tens of thousands of sales people, most of whom only stay in the job for a short time, it's just not cost effective to drag them all up to the corporate training centre to explain the finer points of the psychology of sales. It's much easier just to turn the high performing behaviour into an instruction which is then monitored by mystery shoppers who are given a specific list of words and actions to watch out for when posing as a real customer.

If you've passed your driving test then a familiar incantation will be "Mirror, Signal, Manoeuvre".

The incantation suggests this:

But 'real life' requires this:

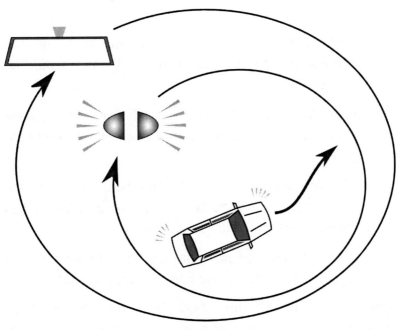

Your driving instructor probably said something like, "But keep checking your mirrors", to make up for a shortfall in the incantation. To be fair, the Highway Code does say that you should keep checking your mirrors throughout the manoeuvre to make sure it's still safe.

The mobile phone company instructs its sales people to do something else too, which is very interesting. When you ask about a particular model of phone, they don't give you a demo model, they ask you which colour you would want if you bought it, and they then fetch a brand new phone. They sit down, cut the security tape from the box, open it, assemble the phone and then hand it to you. But they don't just throw it across the desk, no. They hand it to you using *both hands,* like a Chinese businessman would hand over a business card. A number of very peculiar things are happening in this transaction, including:

- You choose your colour at the start of the transaction, rather than at the end which would be more usual

- You are led to think that the sales person has gone to a lot of trouble to open a brand new phone for you

- You are made to feel guilty that they can't now sell this 'used' phone to someone else because it has been taken out of its packaging

- The 'two handed pass' implies that the phone is of great value, something precious and special

How do I know all this? Because I was that mystery shopper, and all of these cues were in the instructions for the visit. Rather than teach the sales people the underlying principles, it's easier just to send each store manager a set of instructions and then monitor the sales people to make sure they're following them.

This method keeps the costs to a minimum, but the results will be unreliable. The company perhaps sees it as a 'numbers game', where their high profile TV and press advertising creates a steady flow of people through the shop doors, and if the clumsy techniques work with 1% more people, that means increased turnover. It doesn't matter if the majority of customers stare in disbelief at the sales person handing over the phone, thinking, "What are you doing? It's a phone not the crown jewels!"

You can create mnemonics and checklists for the talents that you model, but you cannot use those mnemonics as the foundation for installing the model into other people. The checklist must emerge from the installation process rather than defining it.

The two handed phone pass is a ritual, a prescribed action which is believed to lead to a desired result.

A scripted statement such as, "So, can you see yourself sitting in..." is an incantation, a magic spell which will command the customer to part with their hard earned cash.

But rituals and incantations do not belong in a 21st century, buyer-aware, sophisticated sales process. They belong ion a cargo cult.

Wikipedia defines a Cargo Cult as "... a religious practice that has appeared in many traditional pre-industrial tribal societies in the wake of interaction with technologically advanced cultures. The cults focus on obtaining the material wealth (the "cargo") of the advanced culture through magic and religious rituals and practices.

Cargo cult activity in the Pacific region increased significantly during and immediately after World War II, when the residents of these regions observed the Japanese and American combatants bringing in large amounts of matériel. When the war ended, the military bases closed and the flow of goods and materials ceased. In an attempt to attract further deliveries of goods, followers of the cults engaged in ritualistic practices such as building crude imitation landing strips, aircraft and radio equipment, and mimicking the behavior that they had observed of the military personnel operating them."

Behaviours such as making follow up calls and encouraging customers to picture themselves driving a new car are not talents; they are the observable results of an organised sequence of thought patterns. They are the signs or symptoms of a talent, but they are not, in themselves, the thing to be modelled. When you teach your sales people to make a follow up call, you are creating a cargo cult where your staff are led to believe that, with the right incantations, success will surely follow.

The distinction is that the highest performers don't *always* hand over a phone like that, or ask that question, or make a follow up call. Follow up calls are targeted, just like everything else that a good sales person does. Not every customer gets a follow up call because a good sales person knows that it is not the call that works, it is the management of the customer's decision process. A follow up call is made to customers whose decisions can be influenced, otherwise it's intrusive and actually puts off someone who may have come back and bought at a later date. As a potential customer, I just feel like I've been processed through a sales technique.

"But, oh wise one", you say, "If I can't teach a simple sales trick that my staff can use with every customer then how do I tell them which customers to use it with?"

And that is absolutely the key to understanding modelling. Anyone can make telephone calls. Anyone can manage a staff rota in a supermarket. Anyone can polish a turbine blade. Knowing how to do these things is not what sets a high performer apart from their average or poor performing colleagues. The star player is not defined by what they do; they are defined by their skill in knowing precisely *when to do it*.

We need to replicate the underlying beliefs and attitudes, not just the tip of the iceberg behaviours. That's why the modelling process looks at the behaviour within the person within the culture to produce a rich, multi-dimensional blueprint for success.

The alternative, to use this modelling process to produce rituals and incantations is fine, nothing wrong with that at all, just as long as you understand that the more you strip down the model, the fewer customers it will work with. Whether you model excellence in sales, leadership, complaint handling, technical design or customer service, the more complete the model, the more widely applicable it is because you are installing both the working talent and the skill which created it in the first place and which will allow it to evolve; flexibility.

Technique Creation

Let's go back to NLP's roots for a moment and take a look at some NLP techniques, as they are each an example of modelling, having being derived from people who were able to solve certain types of behavioural problem. Every technique at Practitioner level is a strategy installation in itself. This is one of the key aspects of NLP as a generative technique, in that every technique:

- Breaks the problem (if used correctly)

- Encourages internal generation of new choices (giving control to the client)

- Installs the strategy (giving the client a new resource for future events)

Remember the NLP presupposition that this relates to:

The resources an individual needs in order to effect a change are already within them

The building blocks for all strategies are already within the person that you want to teach the skill to. When you break the process down into small enough steps, you will be able to teach very complex behaviours, based on decisions which took your role model many years to learn through trial and error.

Let's have a look at how two of NLP's techniques do this; the Swish and the Fast Phobia Cure.

I'll detail those two techniques first, partly because you may not have experience of NLP and partly because, even if you do, I've not met many NLP Practitioners who could do a Swish properly, I'm sorry to say.

Swish

Find something that your client would like to be different which involves some kind of reaction to someone or something, perhaps an instant reaction to a particular person who they don't get on with. You need to track down the precise moment that the undesirable "program" runs, so that might be when they first see the person, or hear their voice, or something else.

For example, if you want to swish a fear of mice, don't picture standing on a chair, make it the very instant the mouse appears. Hold your right hand up in front of the person's face and ask them to put the picture there.

Now create a picture of a desired outcome which can be anything that is different to the "problem". Hold your left hand down and over to one side and ask your client to place the outcome image there.

Put your hands down by your side. By attaching the images to your hands, you have created a visual anchor. With your left hand ready, bring your right hand up into the client's field of vision. Only wait long enough to see the reaction begin, perhaps no more than half a second.

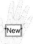

Swap your hands over, quickly growing the outcome picture to replace the first picture as the first picture shrinks away. As the images swap over, make a "whoosh" or "swish" sound.

Swap the images over as quickly as you can, and bring your left hand, the outcome picture, right into your client's face, almost hitting them on the nose.

Hold the outcome image in front of your client's eyes for a few seconds.

Break state by distracting your client and repeat the whole process three times.

To test, ask your client to try to remember the way they used to react to the situation. What seems different?

Fast Phobia Cure

Imagine yourself seated in the middle of a cinema. See the screen from your own eyes and notice the colour of the seats, the size of the auditorium. Be aware of the sensation of the seat comfortably supporting you. Up on the screen, see a black and white snapshot of yourself in a situation just before an experience in which you would have had this response or feeling.

Imagine that you can step out of your own body, see yourself sitting in the front row looking up at the screen.

Now imagine yourself walking to the back row and sitting, looking at yourself in the front row watching yourself on the screen.

Once again, float out of your body, up into the projection booth, so you can see yourself sat at the back of the cinema looking at yourself sat in the middle of the cinema looking at the black and white snapshot of yourself on the screen. In the back row or the projection booth you have to remember that you are not looking at the screen. Only the you in the front row can see the screen, the you in the back row is looking at you in the front row, the you in the projection booth is looking at you in the back row!

Turn that snapshot into a black and white movie running all the way through that experience in which you used to have a response. Let it run all the way to the end and freeze it as a still image.

Remember, all this time you are up in the projection booth watching yourself in the back row. You are not looking directly at the screen.

Installation   236

Now run the film backwards. Run the film backwards quickly, so all the people are moving backwards, all the sounds are played backwards, all the way back to the start. Run the movie forwards at double speed, hear all the high pitched sounds. Play some silly music as a soundtrack to the movie.

Keep running the movie backwards and forwards. When you're ready you can add in some colour and gently slow the movie down until it is running forwards and backwards at normal speed.

When the movie can run, in colour, at normal speed with no significant response, step down from the projection booth and into you in the back seat. Then walk forwards and step into you in the front row. Then, finally, step up into the screen and back into the scene.

Run the whole memory forwards at normal speed, in colour, with sound, and notice what has changed.

15.1 Swish

What is the sequence of steps in a swish? I don't mean the steps in the instructions for a swish, I want you to really break it down, moment by moment.

How does it break the problem?
How does it encourage new choices?
How does it install the strategy?

15.2 Fast Phobia Cure

What is the sequence of steps in a Fast Phobia Cure? Break it down, moment by moment and analyse the processes that are taking place.

How does it break the problem?

How does it encourage new choices?

How does it install the strategy?

Swish

What is the sequence of steps in a swish? I don't mean the steps in the instructions for a swish, I want you to really break it down, moment by moment.

How does it break the problem?
The first movement of hands and the 'whoosh' sound are a pattern interrupt. By triggering the old pattern of behaviour and interrupting it before it has a chance to complete, the swish breaks the problem. It's like the confusion you feel when shaking someone's hand and they pull theirs away just as you're about to grasp it.

How does it encourage new choices?
The triggering event still takes place but no longer leads to an automatic outcome, therefore the person must choose a new outcome in order to satisfy their need to complete the strategy. By swishing in different or even random outcomes, the person must generalise their response to the triggering event which means that their response is no longer automated but is a choice.

How does it install the strategy?
By using the swish multiple times, the pattern interrupt itself becomes part of the new pattern. The person might begin to imagine their old reaction but will stop themselves, perhaps remembering the technique or just making themselves choose a new thought process. When the person generalises this further, they realise that they can interrupt any other 'negative' reactions.

Fast Phobia Cure

What is the sequence of steps in a Fast Phobia Cure? Break it down, moment by moment and analyse the processes that are taking place.

How does it break the problem?
By interfering with the distorted memory of the problem, the technique changes the meaning and emotional response associated with it. These changes, which take place at the unconscious level, make it more difficult to recall the problem as it was.

How does it encourage new choices?
The technique gives the person a new perspective on their problem, and what had been difficult for them to think about now becomes neutral or even funny. However, the triggering event still took place, so the person must create a new meaning and therefore new choices.

How does it install the strategy?
By making multiple changes to the visual or auditory structure of the memory, the person must generalise these changes and realise that it is possible to consciously distort memories, which in turn makes it possible to choose how to distort memories. The person will often then question other troubling experiences and make changes to them.

As you can hopefully see from these examples, one of the most important ways to install a strategy is to generalise it in multiple contexts. Remember my example of teaching children to type more confidently, at home, at school, with friends, with family. In Logical Levels terms, if you only install the strategy at the level of behaviour, it will often be wedded to a particular environment and will not transfer to other situations. A new manager might learn to prioritise tasks at work, but not at home. A new parent might learn to manage difficult behaviour at home but not imagine that they could take a similar approach at work.

As a person generalises a new behaviour, you will hear changes in language which reflect the way that the behaviour becomes part of their capabilities and even their identity.

15.1 Modelling Solutions

Work in a group of three for this exercise.

Model someone who used to have a problem and now doesn't. For example, they used to find it difficult to get up early for work and now they don't, or they used to always overcook boiled eggs and now they get them right every time, or a person at work used to irritate them and now they don't.

Two of you will model how they made that change, all three of you will then turn that model into a technique to be used with anyone with a similar problem.

Remember to test your technique within your group.

At Practitioner level, NLP training gives you a big bunch of keys. You keep trying keys until you find one that fits.

At Master Practitioner level, you learn how locks work.

There are no keys, there are no techniques. Techniques don't work, in the long run. You have to understand how locks work so that you can create your own keys.

Therefore, for you to do elegant and effective change work, here are some simple steps to follow. While they are simple, they are not trivial. Don't be seduced by complexity. Appreciate elegance.

15.2 Custom technique design

Model

Many people just want to rush into a technique because they feel like they're really doing something. You must model, model, model and test, test, test. 90% of your time spent modelling and testing is time well spent.

Only when you really understand the structure of the behaviour to be changed, its purpose in the system and you can test and reproduce the behaviour consistently can you even begin to think about changing it.

Get the structure

Form a representation in your own mind of the structure of the behaviour to be changed - see it, feel it, try it on. Put yourself in there. Visualise it as a machine with real moving parts. Imagine it as a flow of energy, as a road map, as a traffic jam. Find what works for you and stick with it. In essence, you need to make the client's problem real for you. It becomes a shared journey, rather than you just yelling instructions at them from a distance.

Find the weak link

A process is always a sequence, and like any connected series of components, there is a weak link - a connection that is easier to get at, easier to influence or simply easier to interact with.

How do you find the weak link? You test.

Create a 'technique'

Finally, a technique. Imagine the problem as a physical thing, and then think outside of the constraints that define it as a problem. If you see a jigsaw puzzle, where are the missing pieces? If it's a machine, where does the oil go? If it's a traffic jam, where is the short cut? Create a physical metaphor of the solution that complements the metaphor of the problem. Don't think about this, metaphors are unconscious processes. Just go with it.

Do not, ever, under any circumstances, ever, never, ever, try the technique. Either do it or don't do it. Never try it. If you know you're trying, the client won't expect it to work. So either the technique is ready to go, or it isn't. There is nothing in between. The technique doesn't need to be complete or perfect; it only needs to move you a step closer to the client's desired outcome. Often, it's enough to get the client moving, they'll do the rest for themselves.

Test

Now you need to be able to reproduce the solution, the desired response, at will.

Generalise your test through a number of different contexts and future pace in each and overall.

A Worked Example

It might be useful to work through an example in some detail, so I'm going to share a case study of a recent coaching session where a colleague and I worked with a client to create a new method of dealing with customer complaints. The client, let's call him Jack, had endured a couple of particularly difficult complaint calls which had left him feeling shaken and lacking in confidence.

The first thing that we did was to figure out the essence of Jack's problem. We knew that Jack had all of the components parts necessary for effective complaint handling. He could answer the phone, hold a conversation and write things down. No other equipment was necessary for excellence in this task. The essence of the problem was very easy to identify. I simply emulated the behaviour of one of the difficult customers and Jack immediately reacted in a very specific way, raising his hand to his mouth, flushing bright red and experiencing a sudden knot of tension in the centre of his chest.

I find it useful to see such behaviours as purely mechanical responses, as if you're observing a machine and working back through a chain of events. A hand to mouth gesture might indicate that someone is trying to stop words from coming out, words that they want to say but feel that they must not. The knot of tension is a common result of the suppression of an instinct or desire, as if muscles are working against each other, one set trying to act, the other trying to prevent that action, with the result being a tangle of muscle tension.

When I asked Jack about his reaction, he said that it was how his father had made him feel. When I asked Jack what he had wanted to say to his father when he felt like this, he said, "I hate you".

I don't want to look at this in any kind of existential, psychological or spiritual way, just a logical sequence of events, a machine trying to execute its function in unfamiliar circumstances. As a child or teenager, Jack was so practised at reacting to his father in this way that the behaviour, a defensive posture, became second nature. Whenever Jack experiences aggression, he reacts in the same way. Even when driving, Jack reacts to other drivers trying to push into a line of traffic in the same way.

The first part of teaching Jack a more effective complaint handling method is therefore to remove Jack's tendency to shut down and withdraw when faced with conflict or aggression. Getting Jack to verbalise his feelings and say the things that he would never normally say expands his choices and that restores Jack's sense of control. Instead of Jack keeping quite because he can't say what he really thinks of someone, he keeps quiet because he knows it's a more useful choice for him. He could call anyone anything that he wants, any time, anywhere. But as a professional and ethical adult, he chooses not to. Being 'not allowed' to use bad language is something a child would think, not a responsible adult.

With the conflict reaction now dealt with, we started to build a complaint handling process that could be used in any situation. The process was created entirely within the session and was custom designed just for Jack, although as with most models, you'll probably find it will be effective for almost anyone in any situation.

The entire model is also multi-dimensional. Its core purpose is to put Jack in control of the interaction and it does this on a number of levels. At the most obvious, yet most often overlooked level, *any* process would achieve this because the simple act of having a process to follow gives Jack a sense of being in control, of knowing that he would be caught off guard again.

Within the process, each step leads Jack through a kind of 'story' which flows naturally and enables Jack to adjust the pace to the needs of the caller, again putting Jack in control. Then, each step within the process is also designed to put Jack in control. For example, taking notes is just good practice and is something that Jack already did. However, the purpose of taking notes has changed, from recording information to controlling the flow of the conversation. Recording the details of the complaint is the *result* of taking notes, it is no longer the purpose.

As we worked through the process, step by step, we aligned it with Jack's existing skills and experiences. We used Jack's examples and scenarios to create mental rehearsals of each step.

But did it 'work'? Here are Jack's words:

"Well …… I have had to speak to one or two marginally irate parents (although not as difficult as some I could mention!). I applied some of the bullet-point notes that I learnt on the course, and the system worked really well! I must say that having that little list to hand is comforting at the best of times."

A very interesting phenomenon often arises from this kind of work; the client, in this case Jack, goes back to work, armed with their new skill, hoping that a difficult complainer or awkward colleague will give them the opportunity to try out their new approach and see if it works. Often, they're almost disappointed to discover that people seem generally more agreeable than they had before.

Is it a coincidence that their colleagues or customers seem more agreeable? Or has something changed?

Remember that a metaprogram is an organised set of perceptions, and for a behaviour to permanently change at an unconscious level, the perceptions that drive it must also change. Changing experiences and beliefs changes perceptions, and when those perceptions change, the world seems to change too.

Reverse Engineering

Each NLP Practitioner technique is a physical metaphor for a linguistic structure. While those physical metaphors make it very easy to learn those structures at a basic level, they should never be regarded as rituals in themselves, merely as isomorphic practice exercises, which we'll talk more about in the next chapter.

I once heard a Tai Chi instructor say that the art originated at a time when the practising of martial arts was forbidden by an evil Emperor. Monks developed Tai Chi as a way of practising the different movements whilst fooling the Emperor into thinking that they were just exercising for their health. The Monks were 'combat ready', just by practising the component parts of a martial art. Now, this story was most likely made up, and it is more likely that Tai Chi evolved out of a martial art as a keep fit routine. However, the instructor's story is quite nice because it demonstrates isomorphism, as does the exercise of 'painting the fence' in the film 'The Karate Kid'.

Here is a selection of NLP Practitioner techniques which fit this description to show you how conversational interventions have been translated into physical exercises.

Perceptual Positions

This technique is very similar to the Gestalt exercise of having a conversation with an empty chair in order to express emotions towards a person. Most people will tend to only see a situation from their own point of view, and a few enlightened people will see it from the other person's point of view. But I don't think I've met anyone who naturally observed the situation from a neutral point of view and saw both sides of it at the same time.

A Master Practitioner wouldn't need to have people walk to different points within the room, they would create both the dissociation and the reflection at the same time with language such as, "What do you think the other person heard when you said that?", or, "So if I'd been watching this from the other side of the room, what do you think I would have felt?"

It sounds almost too simple, but remember that the modelling process is all about picking up on simple, subtle behaviours. The theatrics of the technique just make it seem more complicated than it is.

Swish

A swish is essentially an anchoring technique, taking a particular stimulus or trigger and connecting it to a different response. The visual perception of a spider is a stimulus, normally leading to a particular response, and the swish uses two factors to overcome this; the first being the timing and the second being the outcome. A visual stimulus happens very quickly, but a kinaesthetic response is slower. By timing the pattern interrupt of the swish at the same moment as the client becomes aware of the stimulus, a second anchor is created to a different outcome. It is important that the outcome is something random and preferably confusing or amusing. All too often, Practitioners are taught to create a 'desired' outcome, and this just locks the client into the same pattern of having no choice over their response. NLP is meant to be generative, meaning that our job is to break problems and support clients to find their own solutions.

A Master Practitioner doesn't need to wave his or her hands in a client's face in order to interrupt a particular response. All they need is good observation and a distraction. For example, if you're talking to a client about their negative response to an irritating colleague, you might try something like this:

"So, sorry, where were we? Oh yes, we were talking about what happens when you're at your desk, the door opens and in walks Fred, what time is it? Because I need to make sure I'm not late for my next session, and you know I was late last week because a herd of cows was loose on the motorway! Cows! Of all things, so there are these cows wandering on the motorway, anyway, Fred walks in, and now I can't get that image of cows out of my mind can you? So tell me how you feel differently about Fred now."

Please, please, don't use that as a script. That would constitute an incantation, and you really must find something that works for you. At the beginning of that example, I had already distracted the client so that they don't get ahead of me when I introduce the image of Fred. The purpose of the hand-waving in the Practitioner swish is to control the stimulus, and you can achieve the same, conversationally, with a bit of planning ahead.

The technique of 'chaining anchors' is really the same as a swish. Chaining anchors is often done with kinaesthetic anchors, whereas the swish is often done visually. You could probably call the conversational version above an 'auditory swish'.

Squash

A squash is a technique that is generally demonstrated either kinaethetically or visually. The kinaesthetic version sets up two physical anchors for conflicting states and then triggering those anchors at the same time. The conflicting states, like hot and cold, can't coexist at the same time, and the end result is a different state which emerges from the integration of the two conflict states.

A visual squash does exactly the same thing with images rather than physical anchors.

But how to do this conversationally? You can't speak two conversational anchors at the same time, can you? You can't say "hot" and "cold" at the same time.

No. Of course you can.

Remember this?

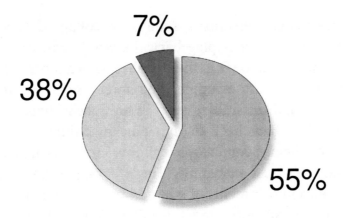

Still in the dark?

One of the most interesting things to do with a client, I find, is to sort their incongruties. There are two types, simultaneous and sequential. Take a look at page 65 and you'll see that one of the requirements for a Master Practitioner is "Sort incongruities and integrate them conversationally."

An incongruity can be sequential; someone says they're hot in one sentence and then cold in the next, or it can be simultaneous; someone says they're happy while crying.

Sorting a sequential incongruity is easy; you just say, "hang on, you said you were hot and now you're saying you're cold. What's going on?"

Sorting a simultaneous incongruity is also easy; you say, "hang on, you said you're happy but you don't look or sound happy".

"Well, I mean I'm trying to be happy because I know I should be, but I find it so hard to keep a brave face".

To create a conversational squash, or collapsed anchors, all you have to do is play back the words which anchor one conflict state with the tonality which anchors the other. In the last example, you might say, "So you're really sad and miserable, yes?" in an upbeat, happy way. If you play them back in the same modalities, you just reinforce them. Some people call this 'crossover matching' or 'multi-channel matching'. That's a rapport technique. It's the reinforcement of the different communication channels as anchors, and the mixing up of them which makes the squash work. And remember, the most important thing with any anchor isn't intensity, it's timing. A Master Practitioner won't separate and anchor the states and build their intensity, they will pick them up mid-conversation, collapse them discreetly and resolve them as they go rather than making a big deal out of them. At the end of the conversation, they client won't remember and 'techniques', but they will feel more at ease with what had been troubling them.

Timeline

Time is a matter of perception. As far as our senses are concerned, time is irrelevant, it's always now. But our evolved brains can do two remarkable things, and scientists still don't agree on how, or more importantly, why. With our wonderful brains, we can remember, and we can imagine.

I have a theory, as you would probably expect. We possess a memory to enable us to plan ahead. By remembering things that happened in the past, we can generalise causal relationships and make useful predictions which are likely to keep us alive.

In today's society, we have learned to use these abilities in order to create, to build cities, to paint, to build complex machines and realise achievements that would leave our ancestors speechless.

The collection of techniques known as 'timeline' are simply anchors for submodalities. A Master Practitioner wouldn't need to get someone to pace up and down the floor, or say, "Visualise yourself floating up above your timeline". A Master Practitioner will, for example, point to the client's imaginary past, present and future and use gestures and language to direct the client's attention to particular points in time.

The traditional timeline technique, where you walk up and down an imaginary line on the floor, is a very useful one, and you can achieve the same results conversationally because many of the words that we use to describe spatial relationships are also used to describe relationships in time:

Near   Far

Long   Short

Forwards   Back

We even say that we are in the "here and now" as we centre ourselves, both in space and time.

¹⁶Instructional Design

The design of a 'training course' is an important part of many installation processes. A number of different instructional design methods exist, ranging from the strict, script based approach through to a more flexible, outcome based approach.

For our purposes, it doesn't really matter which method you prefer to use because there are some useful principles to bear in mind which will make the installation process more effective.

Nesting the Model

A model will usually be a sequence of steps, and it is important that your training design follows the same sequence.

Let's say that you're teaching travel agents how to sell cruise holidays. Using this modelling approach, a well known holiday company modelled its highest performing agent and found that he did something very different to the average agents. Rather than checking availability at the end of the call after talking about the itinerary and so on, he checked it at the beginning. He didn't sell the caller a holiday, he sold them *their* holiday, in *their* cabin on *their* cruise.

So let's design a training course for travel agents which incorporates the model.

We start with a re-enactment of an 'ideal' conversation. It might be done by the trainer, or the trainer might play a recording of such a conversation with a real customer which had previously been recorded 'for training purposes'. Don't explain anything about the call for now, just play it and allow the learners to take in whatever they can. What you're aiming to achieve is to give them an overall sense of the call; the tone, the attitude, the pace and so on.

Now we break the call down, step by step. Take the learners through the procedure for taking a call and operating the telephone system at the point in the process when they would answer the call. Get them to practice answering a call – just the introduction.

Next, get them to take some details from the caller. Their name. Their phone number, so you can call back if they get cut off. And to save them time in case what they want is fully booked, ask which cruise they're calling about. And which dates. And what kind of cabin would they like? Ah, a balcony. Beautiful. Well, cabin 401 is available so now I can answer all of your questions.

It's time to give the learners their product knowledge. The features of the cruise, what facilities are on the boat, the itinerary etc. Have them practice the introduction, then move into the questioning.

What's next? Payment details perhaps? This will no doubt require some more procedural training around the payments system, so now's the time. And how do they practice using the payment system? That's right – they practice the introduction, leading into the questioning, and then into the payment process.

Each time they practice, they rerun the whole model up to that point. Everything that they do follows the same sequence, and everything that the learn comes at the same point as it would in the live call.

If there are connecting flights, which airports? Luggage allowances? Door to door pick-ups? Insurance? Dietary requirements? All of these are now closing details, the necessary points to cover off to complete the booking.

Note that there have been no clumsy trial closes, no, "So if you are happy with the holiday that we discuss, will you be going ahead today?", nothing that seems out of place. No peculiar handing over of mobile phones. No, "So can you see yourself enjoying one of our cruises?"

The high performer placed the customer in *their* cabin on *their* cruise at the start of the call, and that created the frame of reference for the entire conversation.

The training design reinforces the model by nesting it as many times as possible within the training session.

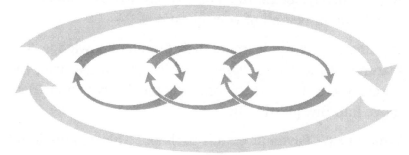

Naming

Use course and exercise descriptions that complement the model and presuppose success. For example, in sales training, the term 'cold calling' is often synonymous with an undesirable and difficult activity. Instead, choose a title which implies that the learners will be calling someone they haven't spoken to before and asking for something; a task that most of us perform every day.

Mnemonics

This next point is really just good training practice, but I feel it's worth mentioning.

Instead of telling the learners what the mnemonic is, have them create it. But like any good magician, use forcing techniques to ensure they end up with the mnemonic or acronym that you had printed on the hand-out cards.

"OK, so what's the first step"

"Find out which cabin they want"

(Write that on the flipchart, but leave space above it)

"That's important, does anything come before it?"

"Answer the phone!"

"Yes, good. Obvious but important! What's next?"

"Introduce yourself and take their contact details in case they get cut off"

(Write those three steps above the cabin selection step)

"Great, what next?"

And so on. Once you have the steps mapped out, and you've paraphrased the group's answers so that the words just happen to spell out the mnemonic, you can do the 'reveal' of the flipchart that you prepared earlier.

This approach is important because by getting the group to create the mnemonic, you are actually forcing them to rerun the model in their minds, over and over as they break it down and search for each step. Their recall of the mnemonic and the steps of the process will be far higher when they understand what's going on behind the process, and you avoid creating an incantation, which is what tends to happen if you impose your own mnemonic. Most importantly, the mnemonic itself comes at the end, an output of the learning process, not at the beginning. Whatever you do at the beginning creates a frame of reference which constrains everything that happens afterwards.

Multiple Methods

You are unlikely to install a model effectively by using one method alone. As with any other learning experience, the more ways that you can engage the learners the better. Here are some ways in which you can do that:

- Talk through the model

- Have the learners physically walk through the model

- Have high performers talk about what they do

- Have the learners read case studies

- Take the learners on a site visit for a live case study

- Have the learners 'role play' through the model

- Create games and exercises which are themselves models of the model (isomorphic exercises)

- Have the learners create the model for themselves

- Observe practice and give real time feedback

- Use guided visualisations

- Show film scenes which convey the attitude of the high performers

- Have high performers 'buddy' the learners

- Have high performers mentor the learners

- Coach the learners using a coaching framework based on the high performance model

- Have the learners create metaphors for the model

Many of these ideas will be familiar to you, so I'll just expand on a few which may not be.

Walk Through

Write the steps of the model on pieces of paper and arrange them on the floor in a line or circle, whichever is appropriate. Have the learners physically step through the model, at each stage explaining what they are doing, what they are thinking, what might happen, how they might respond and so on.

When you use a physical exercise in this way, you will see people embodying their internal experiences. They will play out their comfort zones and fears, regardless of what they say. For example, if the model is a sales process, you'll see someone stop at the cold calling step as if they're standing at a cliff edge. They literally play out what they are creating in their minds. You might also see them linger in the needs gathering stage because that involves talking at length with the customer; the part they enjoy most. By reflecting back such reactions, you can increase the learners' acceptance of the model, coach them through any personal barriers and give them a multi-sensory experience of 'stepping through' it.

Isomorphic Exercises

An isomorphic exercise is one where a seemingly unrelated activity bears a structural resemblance to the model, thereby encouraging the learner to generalise their experience which embeds it more effectively and makes the learning accessible in a wider range of situations. When you deliver an isomorphic exercise correctly, you'll hear your learners say, "Ah! This is just like..."

For example, let's say that you want to install Jack's model of complaint handling. One of the key steps in the model is the taking of notes, because it serves as a 'flow control' mechanism whilst also signalling to the complainant that you take their complaint very seriously.

Let's say that you want your learners to practice writing notes verbatim, because in complaint handling, it's very important to be factually correct and not change the complainant's words.

Make an audio recording of an angry complainant, speaking too quickly for the learners to write down their words. Put the recording on a computer or a tape so that the learners can control the conversation with the pause, rewind and play buttons. Focus their attention on the overt purpose of the exercise by having them check each other's transcripts and awarding points or prizes for the most accurate.

When you set the exercise up, position it only as a note taking activity, but when you later move onto a face to face interaction exercise, point out that taking notes, and the interpersonal skills required to do so, are the equivalent of the pause, rewind and play buttons. By practising first on the recording, you take away the stigma attached to interrupting the complainant and not wanting to appear rude or inflame the situation, and by then reintroducing the concept later on, the learners have already practised the mechanism. The learners will learn to take notes more effectively, because there was no interpersonal barrier of having to interrupt another person, as there would be in a pairs or group exercise. The learners are completely free to hone their note taking skills, and we'll add in the interpersonal skills later on.

This achieves the following outcomes which are each characteristics of the high performer's approach:

- Separate the flow control mechanism from the emotional stigma of interrupting the complainant

- Take notes to record the complainant's words verbatim

- Take notes to signal the complainant's importance

- Take notes to control the conversation, stick to the facts and prevent emotion from taking over

Now, you might wonder what makes an isomorphic exercise so special. After all, separating out the note taking from the interpersonal skills is logical, isn't it?

Firstly, how many trainers do you honestly think would separate the two? Isn't it more likely that most trainers would have the learners practice note taking with each other, because that's just easier?

Secondly, there are lots of ways that you could have your learners practice note taking. What is special is that you have chosen a practice exercise which uses a number of metaphors for the approach that you want them to take in handling a complainant. The metaphor works both ways; controlling the recording is 'like' controlling the complainant, and treating the complainant factually and objectively is 'like' pressing play, pause and rewind without worrying about how the tape recorder feels about it. When you install the complete model effectively, you don't have to install any incantations for reassuring the customer, such as "Your complaint is important to us", because the complaint handler demonstrates that the complaint is important. They don't need to signal to the complainant that they care, because their whole attitude to the interaction is one of concern and care. If you teach a disengaged, disinterested car salesperson to say, "So, can you see yourself..." then the harm caused by the incongruence far outweighs any statistical benefit of the incantation. A disinterested and sarcastic complaint handler will damage your business far more than the product or service issue that the complainant is contacting you about. Good complaint handles have an attitude which clearly signals:

- We're not perfect but we want to get better

- I'm grateful that customers make the effort to give me feedback rather going to our competitors

- We won't get it right every time

- My job is to listen, not to judge

- Without customers, we wouldn't have a business

- I will concentrate on the facts, hear all sides of the issue and put right what we've done wrong

- There are some problems that are outside of our control

- The customer is always right, but that doesn't mean they automatically get their own way

- One unhappy customer impacts our business more than a hundred happy customers

Remember, of course, that a high performing complaint handler does not use their notes as a barrier, because that will frustrate the complainant further. The high performer uses their notes as an *enabler*. How do they achieve this subtle but vital difference? Because it's important that you understand that the tiny difference between the two means the difference between installing an effective model and creating a cargo cult with its rituals and incantations. The difference is that the high performer doesn't shut the complainant out while they take notes; they keep looking at them or talking to them. Their focus is on the complainant, not the notebook.

Guided visualisation

The touch typing exercise with the children used a guided visualisation to create a mental context for model installation. Guided visualisations don't have to involve darkened rooms and whale song, they are simply a hybrid of reality and imagination, structured by an external guide. High performers in a company providing home improvements would take the customer into their dark, dirty garage and have them visualise how it would look as a home cinema. The overt purpose was to have the customer select power points, windows, roof style and so on, but the side effect was an amplification of the customer's desire to go ahead with the project.

A travel agent might talk a customer through the layout of the holiday complex, using strong visual language to elicit an imagined experience within the customer's mind, which will automatically fill in the gaps to create a more complete experience.

"So your room is here (marks it on a map of the complex) and as you come out of your door and into the garden, it's really bright and sunny and you'll look across the bay, so you can imagine seeing all the boats with their white sails, honestly it's such a beautiful scene to enjoy over breakfast, and if you turn to your left you'll follow this path to the health club, and here's where you can..."

Is sunshine cold? Is a sparkling blue bay with white-sailed boats a depressing sight?

High performing finance managers in the retailer visualised the operation of a store, using spreadsheets as their guides. High performing project managers and engineers create a visual journey through a technical project, checking for anything they've missed, step by step. You might do the same thing when you're going on holiday, imagining your journey; "Passport, tickets, book for the flight, rental car paperwork, driving license, directions to the villa..."

Whenever you describe a series of physical actions to your learners, you are essentially guiding a visualisation because they are unlikely to be able to make sense of your description without visualising themselves and their surroundings.

For example, if I 'walk through' the following steps with you, pay attention to whatever thoughts you have:

1. Finish reading this book

2. Think of someone who has a skill that you admire

3. Model it at a very simplistic level

4. Pick out the most useful steps

5. Find a situation where you can try out those steps

6. Use exercise 9.2 to reflect on what happens

What did you notice?

Metaphors

When you create a metaphor, you create new mental pathways to the same underlying information. Metaphors enrich the original experience and make it more vivid and accessible, which makes it easier for the learners to apply the model in different situations.

Throughout your installation process, or 'training course', you can have your learners create metaphors, which might be:

- Synonyms for the objectives of the model

- Acronyms and mnemonics

- Examples of the model in action

- Icons or pictograms to help remember the stages of the model

- A modelling clay sculpture of a successful outcome

- A painting or other artistic representation of the steps of the model

- A 'thought wall', where learners can pin notes, slogans, poems, pictures, sketches, cartoons, logos, musical notes, colour codes, diagrams, flowcharts or anything else which comes to mind for them and which they want to share with their colleagues

- A song, play or comedy sketch enacting the steps of the model

Kolb's Experiential Learning

Here are some suggested activities and questions to use at each stage of Kolb's learning cycle.

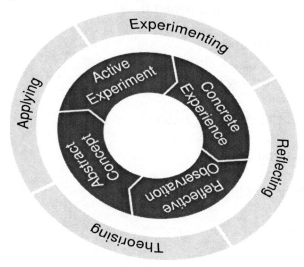

Applying

Work through case studies

Have guest speakers talk about their experiences

Conduct site visits

"What examples do you have of...?"

"Can you think of these issues in your own workplace?"

"When has this happened to you?"

"How could you see this working?"

"Can you think of anyone else who does this?"

Reflecting

"What happened?"

"What would have happened if...?"

"What did you notice"

"What did you say?"

"How did the customer react?"

"How did you feel?"

"How do you think they felt?"

Theorising

"What do you think is happening here?"

"What were the steps that you followed?"

"Why do you think that happens?"

"How do you think it works?"

"How do you think you could change the result?"

Experimenting

"Have a go!"

Keep your instructions simple and direct

Tell your learners what to pay attention to

Other Learning Theories

Kolb's experiential learning cycle isn't the only learning theory. There are many others, including:

- Gardner's multiple intelligences
- NLP's sensory preferences
- Honey & Mumford's learning styles
- Sensory stimulation theory
- Reinforcement theory
- Cognitive-Gestalt theory
- Facilitation theory
- Action learning
- Adult learning or 'Andragogy'

Are these theories mutually exclusive? I suggest that they cannot be. Whatever the method by which we learn, there is no doubt that something starts in the outside, physical world, and is transferred to the inside, mental world as a model. There can be no doubt that these words are not written inside your skull, yet you have learned their meaning, therefore the pattern of neural connections in your brain somehow represents the knowledge which you have gleaned throughout your lifetime, and that generalised representation is a model.

The truth is that we have absolutely no real idea how that happens. Are some people better at learning from images than others? Are some people better at learning physical movements than others? Do adults have a natural desire to learn which must be facilitated? We may never know, because we've lost the instruction manual and, as far as we know, God doesn't offer extended warranties.

However, piecing together what we know by experiment and what we might deduce to fill in the gaps, I suggest that there can be no doubt that learning must have an element of real, sensory experience. Something must happen on the outside which excites our sensory receptors. We must then make sense of that new experience using our existing frames of reference, because what else do we have to rely on? We know that the brain requires a period of rest in order for new neural connections to form, and we know that knowledge must exit in order to apply it. I have to have *some* idea of what to do before I start pushing all the buttons on my new mobile phone or video recorder. And I propose to you that this sequence of events is neatly described by Kolb's experiential learning theory, and the other learning theories listed on the previous page nest neatly within it. How do you like your concrete experience? Visually? Logically? Physically? Musically? Medium rare?

Whichever of these is your favourite learning theory, I encourage you to always make your instructional design as complete and multi-faceted as your learners are.

¹⁷Testing

Testing is important because it completes the cycle that you began with model extraction. If you don't test, you don't really know whether the modelling process was effective or not.

Yet of all the stages, testing is probably the simplest.

To test your model, place your learners in the live working environment. If they get the same results, or similar within an acceptable margin, as the high performers, then the modelling process was successful.

If the thought of releasing your learners 'into the wild' is too scary then there are other ways that you can test them.

One simple way to test is with simulations. I feel that it is extremely important to draw a distinction between a simulation and the perhaps more familiar 'role play'. The two may appear superficially similar, but there is an underlying difference which will absolutely guarantee the difference between success and failure. I would even say that this applies to any training, not just training designed to install high performance models.

When learners engage in a role play, they are asked to pretend that the scenario is real, but at an unconscious level, they know that it isn't. They know that the colleague playing an angry customer isn't really angry. They know that they won't lose their job. They know that achieving their sales target doesn't really rest on this meeting with the Operations Manager of ABC Exports Ltd.

With a simulation, we want the learners to believe that what they are practising is real, at least in the way that they unconsciously respond.

To achieve this, you might construct an elaborate assessment centre. You might have actors playing roles in scenarios which take place before the learner even knows they are being assessed.

Maybe you've seen films where secret agents are trained to withstand torture, the implication being that this is how special forces soldiers are actually trained. Their lives probably aren't in serious danger, but the situation is constructed to make them believe that there is a good chance that it is. Their fear is intended to be real.

Industrial flight simulators are incredible pieces of technology, blending real aircraft hardware, an advanced motion platform and software which can model aircraft dynamics and create real time, photo realistic views out of the cockpit windows. When the pilot walks into the simulator, he or she knows that it isn't a real aircraft. But after a two hour flight, when an engine fails on final approach, their sweat is very, very real. When a pilot 'stalls' a simulator, their stress levels respond just as if the danger of crashing is real. The simulation is so realistic that time in the simulator counts as time in the air for their log books.

But what if you don't have access to such resources? Well, the simplest approach is also the more effective, and it's important to do this even if you do have a realistic assessment centre in place.

I mentioned previously the importance of nesting the model within your learning design. Testing is not a separate phase to learning, it is part of it. In Kolb's terms, the test takes place in the concrete experience stage of the cycle. While the learners are practising, you're testing them, or more accurately, you are testing your own effectiveness at installing a model. Each individual skill that goes to make up the greater talent that you have modelled requires testing in its own right. Note taking needs to be tested. A customer-focused attitude needs to be tested. You can easily test your learners' memory of a sales process, but how do you test the change in attitude necessary for persistence in 'cold calling'?

You could tell the learners that they will be doing some cold calling shortly, and see how they react.

You could use the 'walk through the model' exercise again, this time covertly testing for unconscious resistance at the 'cold calling' stage.

Or, you could make probably the most important instructional design tweak of all; build your training programme in stages, instead of all at once, with periods of real world experience in between periods of learning. I didn't mention this in the Instructional Design chapter because I wanted to use it as an example of testing. Although, to be fair, you should really have worked it out for yourself by thinking about the consequences of Kolb's learning cycle.

Here are two examples of a training day for recruiters who are having problems placing candidates.

Traditional Approach

The training day packs in as much learning as possible, with mnemonics to remember the rituals and incantations, such as AIDA for Attention, Interest, Decision, Action. The mnemonic is defined, examples are shared and applications are discussed. At the end of the day, the learners' retention might be tested, and they might take part in some role plays with scripted scenarios.

Cyclic Learning Approach

The training day packs in as much practice as possible. Theoretical models are sent out as pre-course reading, together with instructions for analysis and self reflection to encourage the learners to engage with the theory. The day is constructed as a series of cycles, with each cycle starting at a different point in the following, just to add some variety:

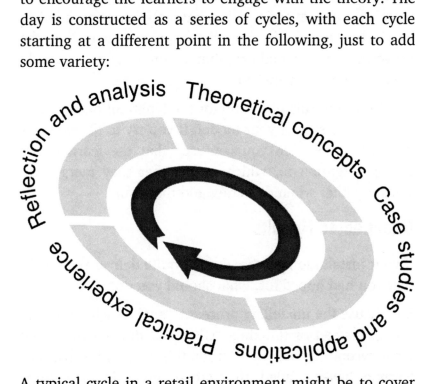

A typical cycle in a retail environment might be to cover some theory about how to approach a customer with some practical examples, followed by some time spent actually approaching live customers, followed by a session of developmental feedback on what happened, followed by some theory on establishing a customer's needs and so on. Each cycle builds on the previous ones, so in order to establish a customer's needs, the learners must approach customers again, now practising the first and second steps together.

Mnemonics arise out of the learning process and represent the theory that the learners abstract their new knowledge into, rather than the theory that they have to learn to apply. If you consider the history of mankind, theorising and experimenting have always gone hand in hand, but if one has to always come first, like the proverbial chicken and egg, then I would say that it would have to be experimentation.

I find that the rule of thumb for the length of one of these cycles is one step of your model. If you try to fit two steps into one cycle then you confuse what the learners are paying attention to, which means that they merge two steps together when reflecting and theorising.

Unexpected Results

If your installation process doesn't quite deliver the results that you had hoped for, what should you do?

Simply use the modelling process to analyse what they are doing. Instead of thinking, "Oh no, it didn't work, what went wrong?", look at it from this point of view. The learners haven't failed, they are simply doing something different than what you intended. Rather than look for what they're not doing, look at what they are doing and compare that to your model.

We've already discussed this in chapter nine, Beyond Simple Strategies, where you learned to ask, "What is it doing?" instead of saying, "It's broken".

I have found that the most common reasons why the installation process doesn't deliver what you intended are:

1. Failure to separate skills into isomorphic exercises

2. Failure to model the beliefs which underpin the behaviour

3. Failure to cross reference the model

Failure to separate skills into discrete exercises

If you don't separate two talents and take the easy route of treating them as one, you'll find that your learner's preconceptions about one skill affects their ability to learn the other.

With the complaint handling example, the high performer exhibits two entirely separate skills, but because they work at the same time, it's easy to treat them as a single skill. The person who excels in this role is able to detach emotionally to control the conversation and yet still communicate that they care. They don't think of interrupting the complainant as being rude, they see it as necessary in order to be of greatest assistance. It's vital that you create separate exercises, otherwise the learners will only learn to control the conversation, with an unpredictable effect on how the complainant feels about the interaction.

Failure to model the beliefs which underpin the behaviour

If you don't pay sufficient attention to the underlying beliefs and attitudes, you will create rituals and incantations. It may seem like a hard line to take, but if your new recruits have beliefs which are too far away from those required to learn the model then you need to move them to something else and hire people who are predisposed to the beliefs and attitudes that you need. We'll talk about the 'talent cycle' later, and look at ways that you can attract new recruits who are already half way there.

Failure to cross reference the model

If you only model high performers then you have no way of knowing which skills are unique to them.

Extremely poor performers are in fact high performers, placed in the wrong environment, so you must disregard them too.

I recommend you always model at least three high performers and cross reference with at least three average performers, and use a full range of metrics to define 'high' and 'average' performance.

¹⁸Evaluation

Believe it or not, I have heard it said by some trainers that Kirkpatrick's four stage evaluation model is out of date and no longer valid. I'd like to explain why it is valid, and how it aligns with the modelling and installation process that we've been exploring together.

First of all, let's hear the prosecution's opening statement.

Kirkpatrick's evaluation method[10], based on research first published in 1959, and even its 'successor', Kaufmann's five level approach[11], is focused on a 'training event', when in fact, learning takes place on an ongoing basis, both actively and passively, and these standard evaluation models do not take into account the informal and social learning which takes place.

Kirkpatrick's detractors cite these alternatives:

- Brinkerhoff's Success Case Method

- Daniel Stufflebeam's CIPP Model

- Robert Stake's Responsive Evaluation

- Kaufman's Five Levels of Evaluation

- CIRO (Context, Input, Reaction, Outcome)

- PERT (Program Evaluation and Review Technique)

- Alkins' UCLA Model

- Provus's Discrepancy Model

- Eisner's Connoisseurship Evaluation Model

So that's that. Learning in this modern age is a cool and sexy thing which no longer takes place in a stuffy old

---

10 Evaluating Training Programs, Kirkpatrick, 1975
11 Kaufman, Keller, and Watkins, 1995

classroom, so evaluation is no longer meaningful. And any theory which is more than 50 years old must be untrue.

Well, Newton's first law of motion is over 200 years old, but it still enables rocket scientists to throw a washing machine at a comet with enough accuracy to hit it head on after seven months of coasting through space.

The problem with this kind of thinking is that it leads to cargo cults. According to Samuel Arbesman[12], we can measure how knowledge changes or decays over time by calculating how many facts within a given subject area are disproven within a certain amount of time. What he describes as the 'half life' of knowledge is the time taken for half of the facts known about a subject to become untrue. When I was at junior school, the number of chemical elements was a known fact; the fixed immutable number of essential building blocks that all matter is built from. The number was 103. Today, it is 118. Similarly, back then there were nine planets in our solar system. Now there are eight. Where has Pluto gone? Has he run away to a better life orbiting another star? No, we have just redefined what we "know" about the universe that we live in.

How does this apply to evaluating learning? Well, saying that the brain is a sponge and when it's full, it's full is a fact. Saying that the brain has a fixed number of cells at birth, and as cells die off they are never replaced is a fact. Both of these facts are now known to be untrue.

However, saying that a person has to learn something before they can use it, and when they use it that action has a resulting effect in the world which can be measured

12 The Half Life of Facts, Arbesman, 2012

is not a fact; it is an observation. And saying that if you want that person's action to be predictable and structured then it would be sensible for the learning experience to be structured is not a fact, it is an observation of a causal relationship between learning and behaviour. And what term might we use to describe an observation of causal relationships? That's right; a model.

Critics of Kirkpatrick say that the first evaluation level, that of the learning experience, is irrelevant. 'Happy sheets', have a bad name because how much a learner enjoyed the training course has no bearing on their ability to apply their new knowledge. Well, I agree with that. I've seen learners have a whale of a time and not learn a sausage. But that has nothing to do with the importance of evaluation, it is a reflection of outcome.

I have seen literally hundreds of trainers in action over the years, and what many share in common is a need to be liked, to entertain their learners. Whatever the explicit learning outcomes are, the trainers have an innate need to create an enjoyable experience. One trainer calls his work 'entertrainment' because he believes that the more entertaining he is, the more people enjoy his courses and therefore the more they learn. Well, like the apprentices in the workshop, they certainly do learn, they just don't always learn what you're paying for them to learn.

Vocational training and even academic education has a purpose, and that purpose must surely define or at least shape the learning process. You may have seen the old photograph of girls in a Victorian school learning to swim. While sitting at their desks. Sitting at their desks, waving their arms in the air, pretending to swim. Now, this photograph may have been taken out of context. The Victorians may have taught children the basic movements of swimming before throwing them in at the deep end, which would be a very good idea indeed. I hated swimming lessons at school, mainly because the water was cold and wet, two things which I would prefer that water wasn't. So a bit of classroom preparation would have been very useful; it may have saved me from ingesting so much chlorine as a child.

Kirkpatrick's first evaluation level is not a test of enjoyment; if trainers use it that way, it tells you that they want to be liked more than they want to educate. The first level is an evaluation of *experience*. The learners may have hated the experience, and that may have been your intention. If your overall objective was "to learn that falling off an unsecured ladder is dangerous" then an unpleasant experience can be very effective. Certainly, we might say that there is no better way to learn the importance of health and safety than to have an accident at work. So the experience doesn't have to be good, it has to be appropriate to the learning objective.

Most of what I've read about Kirkpatrick's model uses the word 'reaction' to describe level one. The evaluation is how learners react to the experience. Are they thrilled? Delighted? Enthralled? Dubious? Confused? All of these are valid responses, but must be judged in the context of the desired outcome of the overall learning experience.

What about the argument that much learning today is informal, unstructured and 'social'? Well, that's true, of course. But it is not an excuse to spend less time in formal training. Informal learning is all very well, but you cannot predict what someone will learn, and when. Again, the apprentices in the workshop experienced plenty of 'social learning', and it was mostly the kinds of things that their managers would prefer they hadn't learned. If you want predictable outputs, you need predictable inputs.

But don't assume that I am blindly in favour of Kirkpatricks' model, I'm not. I simply want to make the point that evaluation is vital at every stage of the learning process, from needs analysis through to practical implementation. Every evaluation stage forms a feedback loop which informs and shapes the entire process. Don't get hung up on which evaluation model is right, just pick one and use it, and most importantly, don't hide behind it. Evaluation doesn't prove whether your training is good or bad, right or wrong, valuable or worthless. Evaluation is an opportunity to test for unintended consequences, an opportunity to see what happened that you hadn't expected and to fine tune your approach to get the results you want.

Instead of saying, "The feedback was poor, the training was ineffective", learn to ask the right questions so that you can say, "That's interesting, the training delivered a different outcome than the one we intended. How can we refine our methods to get the results we want?"

Remember, wherever you are right now is no accident. You have spent a lifetime making decisions and learning from your experiences, and the path that you have followed has brought you right to this point, reading these words. Our journeys have converged on this very moment in time, and by unpicking those journeys together, we really can learn to discover genius at work.

The Beginning

I'll bring this book to a close the same way I always do; with the beginning. When the training event, or the coaching session, or the book draws to and end, it is but one step in the learning journey. Every step is an opportunity to make a choice; either to carry on doing tomorrow what you did yesterday, or to look around you, see that the world is changing and adapt.

Our minds often fool us into only seeing what is the same from one day to the next. Why do today what you can put off until tomorrow? And why rock the boat when what you're doing works so well for you? Yet when you look back through the course of your career, or your life, or your family tree, you see that all of those tiny, almost imperceptible day to day changes created a revolution. And come the revolution, which side would you rather be on?

We're arguably the dominant species on the planet because of our unique ability to adapt, and in adapting, we learn to shape our environment, and that changing environment holds part of our tacit knowledge, passing it to new generations. We learn the rules of the road because they are painted all over it. We learn the rules of office politics because the voices of empires past still echo through the corridors. And with the accelerating development of technology, all of the world's knowledge is just a click away.

Real time access to information, any time, anywhere, is changing the face of learning. But there will never be a substitute for watching a genius at work; a craftsman whose father before him, and his father before him, developed senses so finely tuned that he can measure more accurately than any micrometer and more quickly than any laser guided robot arm.

As we rely more and more on technology to take the mundane tasks out of our lives, we can take more time to sit, watch and listen the craftsmen, artists and masters who are all around us in every walk of life.

This book presents a methodology to analyse and extract those innate talents, a process to refine their essence and share it with others. But, above all else, never forget what those talents represent, and never lose sight of the wonder and mystery that they hold.

²⁰ Appendices

A Talent Modelling Methodology

Culture: Rules, Environment, Marketplace

Person: Beliefs, Rules, Perceptions

Result
Behaviour

Typically, any organisation or team has a number of high performers who consistently outperform the average. It is becoming increasingly common that organisations have two sets of measurement criteria; explicit, task focused criteria such as sales targets and customer service metrics, and implicit, cultural criteria such as attitude, working environment and customer experience.

It is not enough to simply benchmark performance, because that benchmark is a static measurement in a fast moving environment. Managers often say that they have to "run to stand still" in a fast changing business environment, and part of the problem is the use of static performance benchmarks which give the illusion that the environment is changing. In fact, it is easier to harness and direct this natural momentum for change than to create change based on an illusion of inertia.

By analysing a person's ability to get a certain result within a cultural system, we are able to discover not only the person's intuitive behaviour but also the cultural system within which that behaviour works best.

It is very common for companies to hire 'star players' such as high performing sales people and executives, only to find that they do not perform as expected. There was nothing wrong with the person, they were simply used to working within a different set of rules. Some people, over time, will learn the new rules and adapt to them, some will not.

Often, 'culture change' programs are introduced at the development stage of the people cycle, by sending people on training courses to learn the new organisational values. The problem with this is that it is rarely tied into the other parts of the people cycle - attraction and retention - so over time, the 'new' culture works its way out of the system, and the incumbent culture is preserved.

Culture change can be viewed as a natural process of evolution which is itself a learned adaptation to a changing environment. If your business environment is evolving, you need to evolve with it, supporting people at all stages of the people cycle at the same time. By changing the way you attract new people, those people will evolve the culture iteratively and systemically. In the long term, this creates a stable organisation, but it does require commitment and consistency of business strategy, because it will take a year or two for the new cultural rules and beliefs to become 'the way we do things around here'. Also, this is not a one off process. It is important to be constantly adapting and evolving as the market evolves. When companies only run change projects when the gap between their behaviour and the market environment is so big that profits start to fall, it is already too late.

In modelling high performers and using that information to align the people cycle behind a vision and business plan, the result is greater alignment of the culture and the people within it, ensuring that more of each individual's time, energy and commitment is focused on realising that vision.

In a poorly aligned organisation, many people feel frustration as a result of being unable to contribute and make positive changes. Effort is wasted, re-organisations are common and people will disengage and do the minimum work that they can get away with.

Frustration is the physical result of a person's desire to achieve something being blocked or hindered by a barrier which is not under their control.

This situation leads to small negative effects on a day to day basis, and those daily frustrations are compounded over time to lead to a real and measurable impact on business performance.

You might notice that these six levels are the same six Logical Levels which we discussed earlier. I've translated the language of Logical Levels into the language of business, for example the external Identity of a company being recognised as its Brand. You could do the same with any organisation or culture that has its own self-referential language.

Aligning the skills of individuals with the rules and aspirations of the business as a whole encourages individuals to commit their time, energy and ideas. They feel recognised and rewarded because they feel they can make a positive impact.

As each person experiences the sense of achievement that comes from seeing their ideas and desire to achieve being put into action, they want to achieve more. This creates a strong sense that people have control over their personal effectiveness.

Daily successes are compounded over time to lead to a real and measurable impact on business performance.

Modelling

Since we are looking for the difference between a high performer and an average performer, it is not enough simply to model the high performer, because they will share many traits and behaviours with the majority of staff. What we are seeking is the small number of differences that give rise to a measurable difference in performance.

We use a hybrid approach to modelling which generates a model of individual behaviours within a cultural, systemic context and this is the key to our unique approach which preserves the cultural context for high performers.

Installation

The next stage is to install the model into people who are looking for improved performance. Ideally, we need to have contact throughout the installation process to ensure the model is being correctly installed. It is not sufficient to tell people what the steps of the process are, the installation requires an element of experiential learning which must be facilitated to ensure consistent results.

Testing

We need to ensure that the model is correctly integrated into the wider system by testing the model in the live environment. Possibly the most important reason for testing is to understand how the model evolves so that we can build that evolution back into the model.

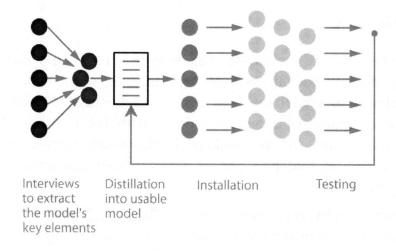

Interviews to extract the model's key elements

Distillation into usable model

Installation

Testing

An Example Modelling Study

This study was undertaken for a major UK retailer as part of the development of their graduate program which prepared graduates for one of three roles in the business. I studied role models identified by HR and business managers and compared them against average performers in order to create the detailed report reproduced here.

The study investigated three roles; store manager, buyer and finance analyst. The complete report was over 50 pages in length, this sample contains only the generic information and the store manager's role.

Some of the results were counter-intuitive and seemed to contradict training previously delivered, such as coaching skills for store managers. In fact, when analysing the results more deeply, what seem like contradictions make complete sense and reveal gaps in the thinking behind other development programs. Feedback like this enabled the client to refine other programs which were in place to ensure they were delivering against the needs of the business.

The result of the client incorporating this work into their graduate program was that they were able to deliver fully prepared graduates into the business after 9 months instead of the previous 12.

Overall, the benefits of this were:

- Saving 25% on the cost of recruiting graduates into the business

- Protecting the unique culture of the businesses

- Ensuring more consistency in the retailer's approach to suppliers and customers

- Improving performance for other staff in the business

- Making future recruitment more precise, effective and economical

This chapter reproduces the modelling report in its entirety, except for the removal of any identifying details, so there will inevitably be overlap with some content that you've already read.

Project overview

Client organisation & business environment

[Client] is a UK based food and convenience retailer. The market environment ranges from large supermarkets to small privately owned grocery shops.

[Client]'s immediate competitors are national chains of small to medium food retailers and also the larger supermarkets in their small format stores.

Business drivers for replicating high performance

In order to establish itself as the leading small format and local convenience food retailer, [Client] needs to attract and retain high performing people into key roles within the business. As part of this long term plan, the new graduate programme is recruiting and developing graduates into three parts of the business; finance, buying

and retail. The future of the business depends on hav
the most effective people in these key roles.

Results and behaviours being modelled

This project is primarily aimed at understanding the key
behaviours of the three roles being modelled rather than
modelling specific, identified skills. Therefore, the first
step is to identify what the behaviours of high performers
are so that these behaviours can be developed into
graduates as part of the graduate programme.

Planned outcomes

A model of high performance which can be used in the
attraction and development of graduates joining the
graduate programme as well as other HR processes such
as the performance management system and also rewards
systems.

Modelling results

The following table captures key information about the
client's cultural environment within which this modelling
project has been conducted.

High performing organisations have a high degree of
alignment between these levels.

Market & trading environment

Highly competitive, fast moving, often driven by price.
Major supermarkets have traditionally driven lower prices
from larger stores but are now moving into [Client]'s
market segment with local convenience stores.

Brand identity

Evolving from a legacy image that was closer to the old [previous retailer] brand to being the leading convenience retailer.

Cultural rules & beliefs

Not as good as the leading supermarkets i.e. higher prices, smaller range, lower availability.

Less negotiating strength due to smaller presence and sales volumes.

The brand is getting better.

Head office environment but not the pressure of London - geography/lifestyle important.

Sense of 'lucky to be here' following the redundancies. Empty office space serves as a daily reminder of this.

Focus on serving the customer through attractive stores and good product availability.

Skills, ideas, capabilities

Open communication, ad hoc meetings rather than using email internally.

Feels like you're working towards something.

People mostly allowed to contribute ideas and be creative, people able and expected to stretch between roles and cover for each other.

Behaviours & key activities

Highly team oriented, clear roles and hierarchy, junior roles analyse data, senior roles make decisions and communicate with the board, clear interdependency of roles, not only work related but also socially e.g. tea making rota.

Stores seem to be driven by executing plans dictated by decision makers and then reporting on the effect of those plans. Again, team oriented but communication seems to be highly variable amongst stores. Some rely on the daily 'huddle', other Store Managers communicate more openly throughout the working day. Again, clear roles and responsibilities. The high performing managers delegate clearly and pass both activities and performance targets down to the people in the store. The high performing managers also create their own clearly defined rules which creates a unique culture in their store.

Working environment

Support Centre:

Friendly

It's OK to make mistakes

It's OK to not know something

Sense of 'lucky to be here' following the redundancies. Empty office space serves as a daily reminder of this

Stores

Focused on availability, customer experience e.g. cleanliness & organisation of store, approachable staff. Corporate procedures are followed as a routine.

Managers create their own rules around behaviour, standards, reward and recognition etc. which can make it difficult for one manager to step into another manager's store.

There seems to be a misalignment between the levels of cultural rules and brand identity. Whilst the new board is working hard to move away from the legacy brand image and market positioning in the same segment as [Competitor], [Competitor] etc., there are still many examples of this focus around the business.

Therefore, much of the business is still comparing itself to [Competitor] and this leads to a set of cultural beliefs that have a tangible influence in buying and retail, and a lesser influence in finance, possibly because of its less direct exposure to competition.

I don't know how [Client]'s customers view the brand, I can only speak as customers when I say that I view [Client] as the business it aspires to be, not the business it wants to move away from. The store renovation program certainly plays a vital role in that. Again, as customers, I can only comment that the store staff play a vital role in brand identity. In the stores run by high performing managers who I interviewed, there was a clear engagement of staff with the processes of running the store. I have visited other [Client] stores as a shopper and not seen this, and the brand that this conveyed was therefore quite different.

There also appears to be a misalignment between the image of the typical customer that drives decisions made in buying and finance and the actual customers in the stores. This is often to be expected as a side effect of generalisation, although I do have a concern that this also represents a change in customer demographic and behaviour which is not yet reflected in the buyers' assumptions.

Role 3: Retail

Results & Behaviour

This section deals with the key behavioural strategies of the role - what the person does, both internally/mentally and externally/physically, to achieve certain results.

Role

The store manager's role seems to be changing as the business evolves. Most notably, the store manager has much less autonomy and less influence over stocking decisions. The high performing store managers use this as an opportunity to devote more of their time to building high performing teams which are not reliant on the store manager for day to day decision making.

Managing the team

The high performing store managers do not manage their stores. In fact, aside from looking for visible signs of the store running as it should do, the high performing manager does not get involved on a day to day basis in the detailed running of the store. Whilst the manager will take time to look around the store, talk to customers, operate the checkout if necessary and tidy up shelves, these activities seem to be based on observation rather than intervention.

The primary focus of the high performing store manager is the team. They manage the team to manage the store.

There are a number of specific ways in which they do this.

1. They use formally recorded data for feedback on store operation rather than looking at the activities directly, e.g. checking the log books for gap analysis rather than checking gaps personally.

2. They create routines for regular tasks which can be packaged and passed to a member of the team so

that the task becomes part of that person's area of responsibility.

3. Interruptions which require their attention will be analysed to see if there is a way that they can be packaged as someone else's responsibility.

4. They delegate the task, the responsibility and the accountability for it, the result being that the person completely owns the task, there should be nothing that they need to go back to the manager for under normal circumstances.

5. When presented with a problem by a member of the team, they push the problem back onto the person presenting it. Only if necessary, they will offer guidance to work out a solution.

6. When giving feedback, they adopt a clear management style, not a coaching style. They give the person or team direct feedback about their behaviour and the consequences of their behaviour. They adopt this approach both for good news and for disciplinary feedback, so they don't ask "how do you think it went?", they tell the person how it went.

7. They spend time out of store, forcing their managers to become more autonomous.

8. They share data on store performance freely with the team and expect the team to understand how they influence that performance.

9. They use the line management structure in the store to manage performance. For example, if a

checkout is untidy, they will ask the checkout operator's manager to give the feedback rather than intervene directly. This appears to preserve the integrity of line management relationships, increasing the staff's autonomy.

Conversely, the average managers were focused on managing the staff, "People in store have the expertise to do what needs doing, I just need to make sure they are doing it"

The high performers manage the staff through feedback data, not by 'making sure they are doing it'.

The two high performing store managers interviewed both had a background in retail and a desire for power and authority. At the start of their retail career, they identified the store manager as the most powerful person and aimed for that role. Now, as store managers, they are both looking for their next promotion.

Their high delegation management style is therefore driven by a need to free up their time to take on parts of their managers' job such as organising meetings, collating report data and managing more than one store. The way in which they free up their time is by packaging their responsibilities into smaller chunks that can be delegated and wholly owned by the person taking on that piece of work. Once they have done this, they mainly rely on performance data as their feedback mechanism rather than looking over the person's shoulder which obviously would negate the time saved by delegating.

This approach extends into day to day store management, where the manager will look at recorded data such as in log books rather than overseeing the activities directly. This is dependent on the manager setting clear expectations about the completion of paperwork and regular tasks, so his or her expectation is that the recorded data is always true and up to date. If this is not the case, the manager speaks directly to the person responsible to remind them of the need to record the information.

Upon taking over a store, there is a period of time within which the staff are getting used to the new manager, so at this stage the manager is very clear and explicit about his or her ground rules and expectations - defining the store's culture. Once this has been established, it is not affected by staff turnover since the existing staff will educate new staff.

In contrast, the average store managers keep management tasks to themselves and do not delegate as much. There is a much stronger sense of the average store being an island, separate to the rest of the [Client] community, within which the staff have their tasks and the manager has his or her tasks, for example:

"There's an awful lot that they get protected from, a lot that I do that they don't have to see or experience because I don't think it's necessary for them"

It's interesting that the average manager thinks about protecting the staff from management tasks whereas the high performer thinks about challenging the staff by delegating management tasks. This results in an average store that is less able to cope with the manager's absence.

It would be interesting to compare store performance to the manager's working patterns to see if there is a connection between the store's performance and the manager's presence. Partly this may be due to a poor delegation style where staff may be more likely to do things properly only when they are being watched, and partly this may be due to a backlog of operational decisions that have to wait until the manager returns.

"The majority of my work's been done today because I was in yesterday" - the high performing manager wouldn't need to come in yesterday to finish his or her work because it would already have been delegated.

The 'island' is also reflected in the manager's awareness of what's happening outside of their store. The high performers knew exactly how their store compared to others, the average manages did not have as much awareness of this.

Feedback and discipline

The establishment of rules and expectations is an important activity for the high performing manager, and it's worth understanding this in a little more detail.

When a member of staff breaks a hard rule such as attendance, the manager tackles the issue as quickly as possible. The manager appears to delegate tasks but to handle discipline issues directly.

The high performing manager reiterates the rules and expectations, and details the consequences of the person's behaviour in terms of its impact on others. This appears to be a very effective way of dealing with the issue.

In one case where the person in question did not change their behaviour, the manager again tackled the issue quickly and gave the person a formal warning. The manager said that he wasn't proud of doing things like that, but the person has to be responsible for their own behaviour, and they have to be made aware of the impact of their behaviour on other people.

You'll notice that this is essentially the same strategy as for delegation - the manager is detailing the task and giving the person the responsibility and accountability for it. If the person fails to achieve the task, the consequences also fall to them.

In delegation, the person who owns the task is responsible for completing it. When they fail they are responsible for the consequences, when they succeed, they get the recognition and praise.

In disciplinary matters, the same is true. The manager makes the person aware of what is expected, why and how it impacts on other people. The person then accepts the responsibility and consequences of either following those rules or not.

If the person changes their behaviour, the change is owned and motivated by them and they get the recognition that they deserve.

If the person does not change their behaviour, they bring the consequences upon themselves and the high performing manager is not slow to act.

The high performing manager therefore creates a set of rules and expectations which are external to the manager. Both praise and discipline are therefore consistent and fair, judged only against these external criteria. This serves to depersonalise disciplinary situations, which I imagine greatly reduces conflict and stress for the manager.

In contrast, the average manager personalises disciplinary situations, leaning on the person's obligation to the manager. This creates dependency and conflict and means that the store team is more reliant on the manager's judgement about the rules. This extends from rules about behaviour and attendance to rules about store operation. This is tied to the average store manager's involvement in the running the store compared to the high performer's desire to enable the store to run itself.

If I also compare the use of management and coaching styles, the average manager coaches much more than the high performer. The high performer gives feedback as a manager - telling the person or team rather than asking them for their opinion - and only coaches when a person has a question about a delegated task. The average manager seems to coach more often, perhaps as a result of their desire to develop their staff.

In one case, an average manager talked about a trading manager who had been promoted to store manager.

"It wasn't me that gave her the chance, she did all the hard work"

This is something that I frequently hear from "life coaches" who attribute change or learning to the client's hard work and say that they only guided the process. In contrast, the store manager is able to take responsibility for their part of the process because they have clearly delegated. In this example, the store manager nurtured the trading manager, so in a way the promotion was the store manager's responsibility. A high performer is happy for their staff to be promoted but sees this as a clear separation of roles with each person doing what is required of them.

Strategy implementation

It was interesting to discover that the high performing store managers will question the timescales or resource implications for an ad hoc task, rather than directly criticising the rationale behind the task itself.

When presented with a task that the store manager doesn't understand or disagrees with the need for, he or she will question the rationale in order to understand it.

Here's what one high performing manager said:

"When you deliver something it's about owning it yourself so if I didn't agree with it initially I would have found out the reasons for it, looked at the benefit then go and deliver it and if I deliver it to my people then I own it"

A very useful and important process arises from this. Faced with an unpleasant or seemingly irrational task, the high performing manager will question it in order to form their own rationale, at which point it shifts from a 'head office' task to a task owned by the manager. This seems to fit with their approach to delegation where they want people to own tasks in their entirety.

For example, redundancy is not pleasant. One manager said, "If these people leave the company then it's safeguarding the company for a lot more people", thereby creating a self-owned rationalisation for the task.

I suspect that an average manager would regard an unpleasant task as being something that "they" want done and questions the task in order to delay or divert it, whereas the high performer questions the task in order to take ownership of it so that it becomes something that he or she believes in and, importantly, may be able to delegate.

Reporting

The high performing store managers appreciate the importance of reporting and they understand the meaning of the data itself. Since the manager is not looking over people's shoulders, he or she uses the formally reported data as the measure of store performance as much as people in the support centre do. In a way, this gives the store manager the same understanding of store behaviour as you might expect the people in the support centre to have.

Preparation and planning

The high performing store managers plan for everything, even for the unexpected. They do this by accepting that there will be interruptions and emergencies, and by analysing every unplanned to event to see if they can turn it into a process or task and give it to someone else.

This is a fundamentally different approach to someone who feels that, as store manager, they are too important to get involved in low level tasks.

The high performing store manager will, if necessary, tackle anything that needs doing in store whilst recognising that fire fighting is ultimately an inefficient use of their time. Therefore they are valuing their own time and seeking ways to achieve more in the time they have available.

In short, by turning reactive tasks into procedures which can be delegated, the high performing manager frees up time to be reactive.

Attention to detail

The high performing store manager has good attention to detail upon noticing an exception but does not get lost in the detail. Starting with a high level of detail, the high performer will notice exceptions such as gaps in availability and will then shift to a lower level of detail, asking questions to understand why something has happened and what is being done to resolve it.

For example, he or she will notice an untidy shelf and will ask the member of staff responsible (or their manager/supervisor) to take care of it. He or she will personally handle anything that is a quick task such as picking up some litter or discarded packaging, but for anything that takes longer than a few seconds he or she will delegate it, which also reinforces the manager's expectations about the task.

For example, if the manager tidies the shelves, how will the staff ever know that it needs doing, and that the manager expects them to do it? The high performing managers are therefore good at reinforcing desired behaviours and giving feedback on performance, which is dependent on their ability to notice what needs doing to a high enough level of detail.

Conversely, the average manager will tend to look more superficially at, for example, the condition of the store. The average manager will accept more inconsistency in store appearance.

Store image

All of the store managers interviewed saw the relationship between the store's image and their own image. The difference was that the high performing managers focused on improving the store and team which reflected on them, whist the average managers focused on improving their own image which reflected on the store.

The average manager wants to be seen to be doing a good job, the high performing manager had a much lower profile and wants his or her store to be seen to be performing well.

The fundamental difference here is that when someone is concerned with their image, they automatically imply an observer. An image is not useful in itself; someone must be looking at it.

Therefore, the average store manager will adopt the ideal behaviour of a store manager when they are being observed, whilst the high performing store manager will adopt that behaviour all of the time, partly because they are the observer of the store and partly because they feel the store is always being observed by the customers and staff.

Let me summarise this important point.

The average manager is concerned with his or her own image and therefore acts as an ideal manager when being observed by someone who they want to convey that image to.

The high performing manager is concerned with his or her store's image and therefore acts as an ideal manager when they are observing the store - which is all of the time.

I suspect that the difference is most apparent in store performance data rather than in direct observation of the managers.

For example, when interviewing one of the average managers, we walked around the store several times. We passed the bread aisle where a loaf of bread had fallen off the shelf and was wedged behind a cardboard promotional display where it was plainly visible. We walked past it three times in total, twice with the manager and once with the manager and trading manager to observe their daily tour of the store to check gaps and store appearance. I didn't mention it because I wanted to see if either of them would - they did not.

Another example: in one of the average stores, there had been some damage to the store's roof and during a period of heavy rain, water had leaked in extensively, damaging stock and leaving a pool of water on the floor. The store staff had piled paper towels around the base of the shelves to absorb the water. The manager said that neither the landlord of the building nor [Client]'s facilities department would take responsibility to fix it, therefore they had to manage as best they could.

I imagine that a high performing manager would not be so accepting of the situation. I can easily imagine either of the managers interviewed clearing their diaries, driving to [Head Office], physically removing the estate manager, taking him or her to the store and doing the same thing with the landlord so that all three of them could meet in person, in the store to see the impact of the damage and negotiate a solution.

The difference? The high performing manager has achieved the position of authority that he or she has sought, therefore nothing that happens in their store is outside of their control.

Conversely, the average manager says, "If you can't influence it you can't change it so there's no point getting upset"

Staff development

It appears that the average store managers believe that staff are inherently limited and unaware of their own potential. Therefore they break down tasks and training opportunities into what they believe the staff can manage:

"It's about giving them chunks that they can digest rather than giving it all at once"

They certainly enjoy developing the staff, the difference being that they appear to single out staff who perceive have high potential and low self belief, and the enjoy nurturing those people. The high performing manager seems to not focus on developing the staff directly but on maximum delegation which challenges the staff and they either step up to that challenge or they don't.

The high performing manager therefore sets the bar high for his or her staff, giving them all a potential opportunity to grow and learn. The average manager singles out staff for development and sets the bar at a level just above the person's own self belief:

"I've got two people who I've earmarked to be trading managers and it's really secretly training them without them knowing it"

The manager in this case believes that if these staff find out they are being earmarked for promotion they will be afraid to take the opportunity.

The high performing manager doesn't single people out in this way, and therefore is not concerned about staff not taking opportunities. The high performer will, however, observe staff performance in respect of delegated challenges and will have a promotion and succession plan in mind. This is different to developing specific people against a predetermined plan.

The average manager tends to identify people who he or she thinks needs a chance to prove themselves or a chance to shine. Certainly with the managers interviewed, a mentor had done the same for them in a key stage of their careers and they now seek out that feeling of nurturing someone else.

In comparison, the high performer's approach would tend not to develop staff who had potential but lacked self belief, so in a high performer's store, some staff may be 'left behind' who would otherwise flourish if nurtured.

Beliefs, Rules and Perceptions

The operating principles and behavioural rules that form the foundation of high performing behaviour.

These are unconscious processes which shape the resulting behaviours and as such are not normally available at the level of conscious awareness.

Behavioural rules

Procedures	Creates procedures where non exist to increase the autonomy of store staff
Towards	Goal and result oriented
People	Achieves tasks through relationships
Team	Regards store management as a team effort, but does not lose self in the team, maintains individual responsibilities
External	Feedback and information driven, sees

	results in staff and store performance
Difference	Notices exceptions that may impact on the smooth running of the store
Active	Takes action early, especially to turn interruptions into tasks which can be delegated
General	Seeks out high level information then drops down to the details for exceptions such as gaps or missed KPIs

Beliefs

The store staff can step up to any challenge or task

Routines and processes are key to consistent performance

People don't need watching but they do need direct feedback

"Retail is about fighting for the customer"

"Some people have got the capability but not the confidence, some have the confidence but not the capability" (i.e. self confidence is the key to career progression)

"When you deliver something it's about owning it yourself"

The high performing store managers had followed a similar career path to that of the buyers; working in a supermarket whilst at school or university, and seeking greater power and authority. The difference was that this group identified the store manager as the most influential person in the business rather than the buyer.

It seems that many people, at the start of their careers, develop a great deal of respect for a particular person who you might regard as a mentor. The high performing store managers identified their first store manager as someone they could respect, and they identified that manager as having authority and control.

In contrast, the average store managers identified someone else as their early mentor, and I found an interesting correlation between that mentor and the manager's career aspirations and the way in which they manage their store.

The average managers did not have a background in retail but were identified by a store management development program as having the potential to be good managers. I think that they are good managers, but they are doing the job of managing, they did not spend their lives in pursuit of the position of store manager. Therefore they do what is required of them, not what they personally believe in.

At an early age, the high performing managers formed a future self image of themselves as store managers. As their careers have progressed, they have shaped themselves into that idealised image. Their drive for greater authority and responsibility has caused them to move that self image on so that it is now of themselves as regional managers.

Conversely, the average managers formed a future self image of themselves in a different role than retail store manager. They too shaped themselves towards that role but found themselves working in other roles. Whilst there was enough overlap between the two to ensure their performance in the role was good enough, it was rarely aligned with their personal identity. You can hear this in people's language in phrases such as, "It's not really how I see myself".

The average store managers can therefore perform well if there is sufficient overlap or if they can mould the store manager's role to the key aspects of the self image. For example, if their self image is of a trainer, educating and sharing knowledge, then they will focus on that aspect of the job. They will want to nurture and develop staff but the store's operational standards may slip.

Another way to look at this is that they are good managers, they are not necessarily retail managers. I believe they can learn to be, but they have framed the requirements of the job through the belief that they were hired for their good management skills and the non-retail experience that they can bring to the role. Combine this with their low exposure to other managers on a day to day basis and they have neither the incentive nor the information to make the shift from being good generic managers to being good retail managers.

"By coming across to retail I was keeping all of my management skills I was just using them with a different product"

"Retail is retail"

Does this mean you can only hire store managers who have worked in retail forever and who have always aspired to be store managers? No, it means that you have to get retail into the blood by creating the desired self image. Graduates need to be inspired by retail, not just programmed to serve. I believe that the high performing store managers would be ideal people to inspire the graduates.

Conversely, hiring only store managers who have a desire for promotion and authority then creates a future problem of too many store managers applying for too few regional manager jobs.

One store manager thought that not all store managers were interested in promotion and wanted to stay as store managers, I wonder if this is instead a lack of self belief on their part.

In any hierarchical organisation, a desire for greater responsibility will always drive the person 'up' the hierarchy in search of more of what they desire. This can create a number of effects, for example that you accept a natural turnover of store managers who become frustrated at the lack of promotion opportunities. At the other end of the scale, if you have only just enough high performing store managers for the available promotions then the result is a significant number of stores with average managers.

In the retail business, there is a budget for waste, as if it is accepted that in order to maintain availability there must be over supply. Perhaps the same approach works within the HR operation too.

Culture

The cultural rules that provide the foundation for the individual high performing behaviours.

These cultural elements describe the environment around the role being modelled and are in addition to the corporate cultural elements described elsewhere.

Each store appears to have its own unique flavour of the [Client] culture. If we regard culture as 'language plus rules' then we have a combination of the [Client] language with the unique behavioural rules of the store.

This seems to cause some problems when a store manager steps in to manager another store. The conflict of rules and expectations can cause store performance to fall, even though both the store and the temporary manager normally perform well.

Retail - the difference

The difference between high performing and average store managers which stands out most clearly is their desire to create a self sufficient store.

(Note to readers of this book: Don't assume that all retailers want self sufficient stores, this is a cultural quirk where a more 'hands off' head office approach creates a void that some store managers step into, creating an environment which just happens to deliver against key business metrics. This would not work in a more centralised culture, and is a good example of a complex set of behaviours arising from an attitude within an environment.)

For years, management development training has taught delegation skills, but that is not what is happening here. The high performing manager does not focus on delegation - he or she focuses on creating a self sufficient store and delegation is simply one means to achieving that.

The high performing manager is focused on results, leaving staff to make judgements on what activities best achieve those results.

The high performing manager delegates in order to free up time, whereas the average manager delegates for other reasons such as staff development. The average manager is selective about what he or she delegates, based on their perception of the staff member's ability. In order to delegate for the purpose of staff development, the manager has to monitor a person's performance and give feedback, which takes time and negates the benefits of delegation.

The high performing manager sets a challenge and expects everyone to rise to it. The average manager focused on developing individuals who they perceive will benefit from development.

It's almost as if the high performers believe that their staff are inherently capable, whereas the average manager believes their staff must be developed in order to become capable.

The average manager is concerned with their self image and since an image presupposes an observer, observation is the driver for their behaviour. At one end of the scale this means they only perform as a manager when being observed or measured. At the other end of the scale this means they perform as a manager all the time in case someone visits the store to observe them.

In order to create a self image you have to put yourself, mentally, in the position of an observer and look back at yourself. This means that the self image will always be an idealised past or future representation - a snapshot of yourself as you were, or as you imagine you will be.

Since the average managers interviewed did not always aspire to be retail managers, they have created a future self image of themselves as a competent manager which presupposes they do not see themselves in that role now.

The high performing managers created the future self image at the start of their retail careers. As they have become store managers, they have recreated the self image of themselves as regional managers, echoing their continuing desire for career progression and greater authority.

The high performing managers are also aware of the connection between the store's reputation and their own, and for them this works in reverse. They are concerned with the image of the store rather than their own image, so in this case they are themselves the observer. They see their performance reflected in the store's performance. As the observer, they are always watching and are therefore always looking for ways to systemise and delegate tasks so that the store can become ever more self sufficient.

This frees up the manager's time in two important ways; it allows them time for reactive tasks and emergencies, and it frees up time for them to seek delegation from their managers, preparing them for their next promotion.

Since the average managers do not focus on creating autonomy, they tend to hold on to decision making and only selectively and partly delegate tasks, creating greater dependency. This means that reactive tasks and emergencies are an interruption and create time conflict.

The focus on staff development meant that the average managers spent more time coaching staff whereas the high performers would manage when appropriate and coach when appropriate, and there were clear distinctions between the two.

One of the high performers said, "Some people have got the capability but not the confidence, some have the confidence but not the capability". So all of the managers understood that self confidence or self belief is important in career progression. The average managers saw this is a cue to intervene in someone's career development, the high performers saw it as a way of selecting out people who don't have the confidence to seek promotion.

In summary, the average manager's role is to manage the store. The high performing manager's role is to drive the store to manage itself.

Overall Observations

Culture

Focus around the business on comparing [Client] with the big supermarkets drives a set of associated beliefs, for example:

- We're not as big as [Competitor], and therefore our suppliers don't take us as seriously

- We're not as cheap as [Competitor], therefore we have to work harder to get customers to buy from us

- Our typical customer is a retired person doing a main shop locally and are therefore not as sensitive to price and quality

Most of the people interviewed said that what drew them to [Client] is the friendly, team oriented culture. Some of the subjects had left or turned down roles in other retailers because of this cultural environment.

Data

The [Client] business generates and consumes huge volumes of data. This appears to serve the aim of presenting every customer with exactly the products they want at the time the walk into the store, and also enticing them to buy more than they had come in for, or to try new products that complement what they came in for.

Of course, the stores cannot be rearranged and stocked to suit every individual customer, so the data is generalised to create a 'typical' customer. In store, the primary focus is availability, so the stores aim to have as much stock as possible, but not too much, of the products that they are instructed to sell.

New product decisions are made on the basis of data, some of which is historical and some of which is based on trials. Therefore since data is collected from sales, decisions are primarily driven by customer behaviour.

I imagine that a consequence of this is that the data you collect from sales always confirms that you sell what you have available, so it makes it harder to change the retail strategy based on gathering sales data. The new retail strategy around the availability of core products seems to be a focusing of strategy rather than a change.

In a positive sense, this means that you always respond to the needs of your customers. On the other hand, it means that you tend to reinforce the customer profile and behaviour that you have had in the past rather than identifying the types of customers you want in the future.

There seems to be a widely accepted belief that [Client]'s typical customer is an older or retired person who shops locally because they can't or don't want to travel to a [Competitor] or [Competitor] and are therefore less sensitive to price and brand. If this is indeed the typical customer, then this potentially creates the problem that [Competitor] suffered; that the target market is shrinking.

Conversely, some of the interview subjects told me that in City Centre stores, the typical customer is a professional commuter, stopping for a top up shop on the way home. Certainly on our visits to stores, both for interviewing and for shopping, I have observed that the older typical customer makes up the minority of shoppers. Our point is that basing strategic decisions on historical data - even data from only a week ago - will tend to root the organisation in the past. This is neither good nor bad, you must simply ensure it is aligned with your strategy.

When the finance analysts provide a report on the viability of a new product range, the decision is based partly on historical data which shows that the product hasn't sold in the past. This leads to a decision based on the summary, "This won't work because...", which can lead to a risk aversion culture, which in an uncertain environment is not necessarily a bad thing. The alternative is to ask, "How do we make this work?" For example, how does [Client] attract the customers it wants in the future, rather than how does it serve the customers it has had in the past.

Overall, the culture of the business appears to be highly data driven. There is a reality of what is happening within stores which is turned into data which is sent to Bristol where it is analysed so that people can turn the data back into a mental representation of what is happening within store. Everyone interviewed in Bristol spoke about using the data from various systems to build up a mental picture of store activity; whether behind the scenes in the management of the store and the supply chain or in the behaviour of the shoppers in the store front.

In short, the decision makers in the Support Centre can't see and hear what is going on in every store, during every minute of every day. They collect data which represents what is happening and from that, attempt to recreate the reality of what is happening in a generalised way that they can apply to all stores. They then make decisions using that data and turn those decisions back into data that can be communicate to stores. The stores take action on that data and as a result, what is going on in the stores changes. And so on.

The NLP Master Practitioner Manual

The diagrams below shows this communication cycle with the three roles that have been modelled mapped onto it.

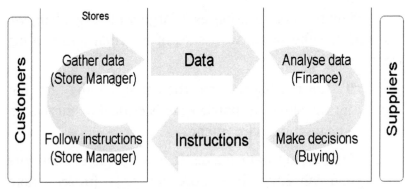

Since every number in every system is gathered from an activity in the business, effective decision making means turning those numbers back into a representation of the original activities.

This is essentially the same process of deletion, distortion and generalisation that is present in human sensory perception where the stores are analogous to the body and sensory organs, and the Support Centre is analogous to the brain. Internal data capture and communication systems are analogous to the nervous system.

This metaphor is important for two reasons:

1. There is always a time delay between data, decision, action and feedback. Shortening this time enables higher quality feedback, more accurate behaviour and therefore better decisions that increase the organism's chances of survival.

2. The process of deletion, distortion and generalisation means that the organism responds, not to reality, but to an approximation of reality

that is only as accurate as the organism's ability to handle the amount of data generated.

If we view the organisation as a large scale organism, we can see that the same two issues of information handling exist.

1. It's not the big that eat the small, it's the fast that eat the slow. Response time is critical to survival in a changing environment.

2. Simplifying data makes it less accurate, therefore you can either hire more people to process more data, or invest in more IT systems to process more data, or base decisions on the most useful generalisation, accepting its limitations. Believing the data to be 'true' is probably the greatest risk of all.

The most notable generalisation is of the typical [Client] customer which seems to drive buying decisions and retail strategy. The question is therefore not how to gather more data on more customers to create many typical customers, but what the ideal customer will be in the future in order to achieve the business strategy. Whilst this is still a generalisation, it is one which guides organisational responses towards the future rather than into the past.

When limited IT systems were available to analyse data in the past, the key problem seems to have been generalisation, for example what products were popular in a store in Eastbourne were not the same as those for London or a petrol forecourt. Greater granularity of data addresses the problem of generalisation, but it creates another - information overload.

This was particularly evident amongst the buyers who make decisions almost entirely on the data presented. There are too many factors to take into account, so they appear to make decisions based on immediately available data and then tweak their decisions based on subsequent findings. Clearly, the more experience a buyer has of his or her product area, the more informed these decisions are. They certainly seemed to base stocking decisions on a small number of criteria which in turn represented a broad base of product and retail knowledge.

For instance, to stock a new product means to take another product off the shelf. Apart from the sales data of the product that will go out of stock, it seems very difficult to analyse all of the consequences of the decision, so the approach taken appears to be to do it anyway and then wait for the data to show the effect of the decision when the decision may then be reversed.

Whilst this broad knowledge may seem difficult to replicate within the graduates in a short space of time, we should remember that there is sufficient data generated within the business to allow anyone to make these decisions because the cause of making, for example, a change to the ranging priority of a product is the sales data itself.

Deletion and distortion seem to be less evident in the communication chain. In particular, the honesty of the finance teams was interesting. They appeared to be happy to present good or bad news as long as the quality of the analysis was not in question. Therefore, they are not inclined to present the numbers that people want to see; they present the numbers as they are. The only issue with this is that the numbers as they are may not reflect the future direction of the business as I have mentioned previously.

The board's shift of focus from chasing [Competitor] to being the leading convenience retailer doesn't seem to have reached all parts of the organisation. Prices are compared to [Competitor]'s, mainly because it is easy to gather [Competitor]'s prices electronically. The stores compare their offers to [Competitor]'s and the buyers compare their buying power to [Competitor]'s. Clearly [Competitor] has dominated the retail landscape, both amongst its customers and with the general public through its huge media presence.

If I were advising on retail strategy, I would be suggesting that you need to focus more, right across the business, on the convenience market and leave [Competitor] to fight their own battles. You need to find your own niche and stick to it rather than confusing the issue with any mention of [Competitor]. For example, the buyers don't think they have the buying power of [Competitor], however it is not in the interests of manufacturers to increase [Competitor]'s market share. Instead of feeling second best to [Competitor], the buyers should be driving the point that, as the leading convenience retailer, [Client] is in a unique position that [Competitor] will never occupy. I still believe that the local presence and the personal relationships between staff and regular shoppers are key to [Client]'s success. As new entrants such as [Competitor] come into the market, I suggest that

[Client] risks being caught in the middle market; not the cheapest, not the biggest, not the most expensive, not the smallest. Historically, companies that are caught in the middle of a market struggle to survive, unless they create a niche.[13]

In talking to the store managers and asking them what they think a typical customer is, they echoed our own observations in store - there isn't one, at least not in social demographic terms. The typical [Client] customer appears to be 'someone who lives locally' and again I would suggest that this is your key strength which you can still do more to build upon.

But since I'm not advising you on retail strategy, I won't mention it.

There is one more important point about basing decisions on current sales data - you only know what customers are buying, not what they are not buying.

One of the buyers mentioned a specific flavour of a product and said that it isn't stocked because the typical [Client] customer doesn't understand what it is. When I was in one of the stores talking to the manager, a woman of about 70 asked for that specific flavour and was told it wasn't stocked. She was exactly a typical customer, according to the generalised model, and she certainly understood the flavour. It's easy to say this is an isolated case and you can't stock every product that everyone wants. On the other hand, what are the chances of a buyer mentioning that flavour and on the day I was in

---

13 Interestingly, about a year after this report was produced, this prediction came true. The retailer was acquired by a competitor and stores were either merged, rebranded or closed.

store, a customer asking for it? There doesn't seem to be a system for recording this kind of data about what your customers are not buying because it isn't stocked. By basing decisions on what they are buying rather than on what they want to buy, you may be missing important opportunities to develop the brand in line with your customers' changing needs.

Decision making

To an external observer, the organisation appears to be driven in a highly centralised way with the board driving strategic decision making and the buyers driving tactical product decision making. Particularly in the stores, the impact of these decisions was visible, along with the conflict that is sometimes created, for example around task deadlines and workload.

It appears that this highly centralised decision making function relies heavily on data, however the journey that the data takes to get to the board, as described above, may impact on the quality of that data and therefore the quality of the decision making process.

I would define the quality of a decision based only on its longevity. If you find that the decision does not meet your expectations in 'real life' and you have to change the course of action, this is often a sign that the data supporting the decision did not reflect 'real life' in the first place.

One example of this is the new store rota scheduling system. It seems that data has been collected from all store staff in order to categorise their level of flexibility around working patterns. The collection of the data itself caused some workload conflicts in larger stores. Our understanding is that the data will be used to build a software scheduling system which will deliver store rotas based on staff flexibility which takes into account seasonal retail trends.

The obvious downside to this is the time delay. By the time the data is collected, sorted and used to generate a rota, the level of flexibility of staff will have changed and store managers may have to make manual adjustments. I suspect that for a large number of staff, their flexibility is not static and changes around school terms, holidays, health etc. If staff are to be shared between stores then I can see the benefit of a centralised rota scheduling system. Otherwise, it adds delay into what I suspect is a very dynamic decision making process.

I trust that there are sound operational decisions for introducing the system, I'm just using it as an example to illustrate the point about delay in a decision making system.

I would also guess that high performing store managers experience fewer staffing problems and therefore benefit least from the new system. I would suggest that this is due to two key reasons; firstly, communication with staff and secondly an understanding of the retail business and its trends, gathered from their many years in the industry.

Communication

The aspect of culture that struck me most was communication. Many corporate cultures actively prevent communication, for example people who sit a few feet apart will email each other rather than have a direct conversation. In [Client], the opposite was true. Everyone's first thought on raising a question was to physically go and talk to the person with the answer. Of all of the businesses I have worked in and with, this is one of the most people driven.

A regulated business would typically be different to this, perhaps because of the need for audit trails on all communications and decisions. A blame culture tends to drive people and teams into silos, cutting off communication from the rest of the business and causing people to communicate via email so that they don't have to deal with the immediacy of face to face interaction.

Of course, other organisations don't actively block communication, but if you start a new job and receive emails from people who you can see sitting at their desks, you learn that this is the accepted way to communicate, and this is the way that cultural rules are passed on to new generations.

The people driven nature of the business leads to the subjectivity of decisions that I have already mentioned. Once again, this is neither good nor bad and it has both advantages and disadvantages compared to automating decision processes.

Roles, hierarchy and knowledge

In modelling the three people from Finance, it occurred to me that what makes a high performer in a junior finance role may not be the same characteristics that make a high performer in a senior role. Certainly the people I interviewed seemed quite content for their managers to take the responsibility for decision making, and viewed job and industry experience as a valuable asset that they did not necessarily possess. For example, the ability to use their years of experience to make a complex financial calculation mentally and for the result to be very close to the result that came from data analysis.

The downside of this is that it potentially places the decision making responsibility with senior managers, taking [Client] back to the old culture where tacit knowledge was protected instead of being systemised and widely available. The creation of bespoke analysis systems for different teams is a part of this process of knowledge protection, for example Access, Excel, SQL and all of the mainframe systems such as those for gap analysis, product ranging etc. - "We keep all our information separate to the rest of the business because it's quite important"

I believe that from a corporate point of view, it is not a good idea to be reliant on people who can use their experience to make mental calculations, because that makes the organisation highly dependent on those individuals, a situation which appears to have been changed by the redundancies but which may be creeping back in. The issue is not the risk of mistakes but the risk of losing a person with irreplaceable knowledge.

The good news about this for the graduate programme is that the right people will acquire the right experience and will therefore, over time, develop similar abilities.

Recommendations

Self image and identity

Spend some time during the training program getting the graduates to form a future self image which is closely aligned with the business strategy for that role and creates a compelling point of reference for them.

Use role models and mentors to help the graduates identify the qualities which they most admire and aspire to.

Getting the picture

Time in store is highly valuable, not just for giving graduates a sense of what happens within store but to submerse them in the [Client] culture. The more time they spend in a variety of roles in store, the more accurate their mental representations of store activity are likely to be, and spending time in store is something that I suggest the graduates do throughout the program, not just at the start of it.

Recommendations relating to the Talent Cycle

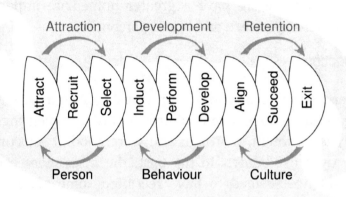

Attraction

Many of the people in buying and retail roles had always worked in retail, starting off 'stacking shelves' and aspiring to a role with more authority, either in store as a manager or at 'head office' as a buyer. The choice seems to depend on where they perceived the power and control being. Therefore, the stores are probably a good place to look for future talent in store management and buying. In finance, it is important to attract people based on the [Client] culture as a friendly, supportive environment which enables a better quality of life than would perhaps be the case at [Competitor].

Recruitment

No data was gathered on the current recruitment process. This year, the graduate programme will recruit 29 graduates. The business as a whole will recruit around 20,000 people. It seems logical to apply the same care to the majority of people that [Client] recruits, especially since the majority of these will be customer facing staff and will therefore have a greater immediate impact on customer experience and brand perception.

Selection

Interview subjects who had previously joined as graduates regarded the assessment centres highly, commenting that they were tough, thorough and were good at selecting in the right candidates. In the past, the assessment centres for finance seemed to have recruited some people who were looking for short term, high impact development of the kind they might get at a 'big four' accountancy practice. I understand that this has now changed.

Induction

The rotation aspect of the graduate programme was again highly regarded. To enable even greater openness and communication between teams, and to protect against isolation of departments, you might consider giving graduates rotation assignments outside of the role that they are recruited into so that they can experience everything that happens in the business and clearly understand the impact of their role on it.

Performance

Other than financial reporting data and business KPIs, I did not see any personal performance data. As a general rule, individual performance goals should be closely aligned with business performance measures.

Development

Not enough data was gathered. The internal development programmes that were mentioned were the CIMA qualification and the store manager's programme which were both highly regarded.

Alignment

Teams seem to be closely aligned around roles and responsibilities. Communication within teams was generally good, awareness of other teams was generally limited to functional relationships. Some teams had regular social activities, some did not. To enable even greater openness and communication between teams, and to protect against isolation of departments, you might consider giving graduates rotation assignments outside of the role that they are recruited into so that they can experience everything that happens in the business and clearly understand the impact of their role on it. Once people are in full time positions, you might still consider even more regular exposure to other parts of the business, e.g. for a finance analyst to visit stores and see the activities that are represented in the data they analyse.

In the stores, the successful managers created their own unique culture. I would recommend building on this, adding in a stronger local element with community involvement, giving managers even more tools to build local 'tribes'.

Succession

Senior roles seemed to depend on a great deal of experience or tacit knowledge as well as a willingness to make decisions. This would therefore suggest that the people who make an effort to broaden their experience and become involved in decisions would be the preferred candidates for promotion, although this may not be fully recognised in the current interviewing process which seems to favour interview/assessment centre performance.

Exit

Since [Client], like many retailers, employs many part time and seasonal staff, care should be taken to manage the exit process so that experienced staff are attracted back into the business as their circumstances change.

Methodology

Typically, any organisation or team has a number of high performers who consistently outperform the average. It is becoming increasingly common that organisations have two sets of measurement criteria; explicit, task focused criteria such as sales targets and customer service metrics, and implicit, cultural criteria such as attitude, working environment and customer experience.

It is not enough to simply benchmark performance, because that benchmark is a static measurement in a fast moving environment. Managers often say that they have to "run to stand still" in a fast changing business environment, and part of the problem is the use of static performance benchmarks which give the illusion that the environment is changing. In fact, it is easier to harness and direct this natural momentum for change than to create change based on an illusion of inertia.

By analysing a person's ability to get a certain result within a cultural system, we are able to discover not only the person's intuitive behaviour but also the cultural system within which that behaviour works best.

It is very common for companies to hire 'star players' such as high performing sales people and executives, only to find that they do not perform as expected. There was nothing wrong with the person, they were simply used to working within a different set of rules. Some people, over time, will learn the new rules and adapt to them, some will not.

Often, 'culture change' programmes are introduced at the development stage of the people cycle, by sending people on training courses to learn the new organisational values. The problem with this is that it is rarely tied into the other parts of the people cycle - attraction and retention - so over time, the 'new' culture works its way out of the system, and the incumbent culture is preserved.

Culture change can be viewed as a natural process of evolution which is itself a learned adaptation to a changing environment. If your business environment is evolving, you need to evolve with it, supporting people at all stages of the people cycle at the same time. By changing the way you attract new people, those people will evolve the culture iteratively and systemically. In the long term, this creates a stable organisation, but it does require commitment and consistency of business strategy, because it will take a year or two for the new cultural rules and beliefs to become 'the way we do things around here'. Also, this is not a one off process. It is important to be constantly adapting and evolving as the market evolves. When companies only run change projects when the gap between their behaviour and the market environment is so big that profits start to fall, it is already too late.

So in modelling high performers and using that information to align the people cycle behind [Client]'s vision and business plan, the result is greater alignment of the culture and the people within it. The result of this is that more of each individual's time, energy and commitment is focused on realising that vision.

This diagram illustrates a poorly aligned organisation, where many people feel frustration as a result of being unable to contribute and make positive changes. Effort is wasted, re-organisations are common and, ultimately, people will disengage and do the minimum that they can.

Frustration is the physical result of a person's desire to achieve something being blocked or hindered by a barrier which is not under their control.

This situation leads to small effects on a day to day basis, and those daily frustrations are compounded over time to lead to a real and measurable impact on business performance.

Aligning the skills of individuals with the rules and aspirations of the business as a whole encourages individuals to commit their time, energy and ideas. They feel recognised and rewarded because they feel they can make a positive impact on the business or their team.

In short, people feel that they are making a difference to their working environment and their colleagues and customers. As each person experiences the sense of achievement that comes from seeing their ideas and desire to achieve being put into action, they want to achieve more. This creates a strong sense that people have control over their personal effectiveness.

| Market |
| Brand |
| Culture |
| Skills |
| Behaviour |
| Workplace |

This situation also leads to small effects on a day to day basis, and those daily successes are compounded over time to lead to a real and measurable positive impact on business performance.

Modelling

Since we are looking for the difference between a high performer and an average performer, it is not enough simply to model the high performer, because they will share many traits and behaviours with the majority of staff. What we are seeking is the small number of differences that give rise to a measurable difference in performance.

A hybrid approach to modelling generates a model of individual behaviours within a cultural, systemic context and this is the key to our unique approach which preserves the cultural context for high performers.

Installation

The next stage is to install the model into people who are looking for improved performance. Ideally, we need to have contact throughout the installation process to ensure the model is being correctly installed. It is not sufficient to tell people what the steps of the process are, the installation requires an element of experiential learning which must be carefully facilitated to ensure consistent results.

Testing

We need to ensure that the model is correctly integrated into the wider system by testing the model in the live environment. Possibly the most important reason for testing is to understand how the model evolves in the live environment so that we can build that evolution back into the model.

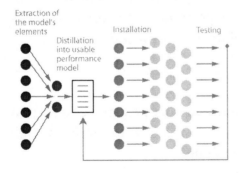

Service integration

A logical extension of this work is to build the model into the HR life cycle. We can apply the modelling data throughout the talent cycle as follows:

Attract

Ensure that marketing and branding are aligned with what the organisation is actually delivering.

Recruit

Ensure that the recruitment process attracts the right people and sets their expectations correctly for the working environment and desired behaviours.

Select

Create profiling templates and assessment centres that select in people who are most likely to perform well within the cultural environment.

Induct

Further refine expectations and align them with the reality of the organisation.

Perform

Create performance review processes that focus on high performing behaviours.

Develop

Create development programmes and coaching frameworks that further enhance performance within the cultural context.

Align

Align individuals into teams and lead those teams in a way that enhances performance and positively reinforces the culture and environment.

Succeed

Plan for the progression of individuals through the business in a way which evolves the culture against market changes and preserves high performance over time.

Exit

Use exit data to adapt the performance model, and manage individuals out of the business in a way that is aligned with the culture.

Further Reading

The NLP Practitioner Manual	Peter Freeth & Stepheni Smith
Structure of Magic, vols 1 & 2	Bandler & Grinder
Patterns of the Hypnotic Techniques of Milton H Erickson MD, vols 1 & 2	Bandler & Grinder
Modelling with NLP	Robert Dilts
The Brain that Changes Itself	Normal Doidge
Growing Up With Lucy	Steve Grand

Lightning Source UK Ltd.
Milton Keynes UK
UKOW04f0642300714

236028UK00001B/71/P